"For I know the plans I have for you,"
declares the L ORD, "plans to prosper you and
not to harm you, plans to give you hope and a future."

—J EREMIAH 29:11 (NIV)

MYSTERIES OF COBBLE HILL FARM

Digging Up Secrets
Hide and Seek
Into Thin Air
Three Dog Knight
Show Stopper
A Little Bird Told Me
The Christmas Camel Caper
On the Right Track
Wolves in Sheep's Clothing
Snake in the Grass
A Will and a Way
Caught in a Trap
Of Bats and Belfries

MYSTERIES OF COBBLE HILL FARM

Of Bats and Belfries

SHIRLEY RAYE REDMOND

A Gift from Guideposts

Thank you for your purchase! We want to express our gratitude for your support with a special gift just for you.

Dive into **Spirit Lifters**, a complimentary e-book that will fortify your faith, offering solace during challenging moments. Its 31 carefully selected scripture verses will soothe and uplift your soul.

Please use the QR code or go to **guideposts.org/ spiritlifters** to download.

Mysteries of Cobble Hill Farm is a trademark of Guideposts.

Published by Guideposts
100 Reserve Road, Suite E200, Danbury, CT 06810
Guideposts.org

Copyright © 2025 by Guideposts. All rights reserved. This book, or parts thereof, may not be reproduced, stored in a retrieval system, or transmitted in any form or by any means, electronic, mechanical, photocopying, recording, or otherwise, without the written permission of the publisher.

This is a work of fiction. While the setting of Mysteries of Cobble Hill Farm as presented in this series is fictional, the location of Yorkshire, England, actually exists, and some places and characters may be based on actual places and people whose identities have been used with permission or fictionalized to protect their privacy. Apart from the actual people, events, and locales that figure into the fiction narrative, all other names, characters, businesses, and events are the creation of the author's imagination and any resemblance to actual persons or events is coincidental. Every attempt has been made to credit the sources of copyrighted material used in this book. If any such acknowledgment has been inadvertently omitted or miscredited, receipt of such information would be appreciated.

Scripture references are from the following sources: *The Holy Bible, King James Version* (KJV). *The Holy Bible, New International Version* (NIV). Copyright © 1973, 1978, 1984, 2011 by Biblica, Inc. Used by permission of Zondervan. All rights reserved worldwide. www.zondervan.com.

Cover and interior design by Müllerhaus
Cover illustration by Bob Kayganich at Illustration Online LLC.
Typeset by Aptara, Inc.

ISBN 978-1-961442-29-0 (hardcover)
ISBN 978-1-961442-30-6 (softcover)
ISBN 978-1-961442-31-3 (epub)

Printed and bound in the United States of America
10 9 8 7 6 5 4 3 2 1

MYSTERIES OF COBBLE HILL FARM

Of Bats and Belfries

GLOSSARY OF UK TERMS

cuppa • cup of tea or other hot beverage

humbug • hard candy

Jammie Dodger • a jam-filled sandwich cookie made of shortbread biscuits

lorry • truck

nappy • diaper

pram • baby carriage

pudding • a general term for dessert of any kind

torch • flashlight

twitchers • bird watchers

wellies • Wellington boots

wind up • tease

windscreen • windshield

CHAPTER ONE

Harriet Bailey's assistant, Polly Thatcher, poked her head around the office door. With a gleam in her gray eyes, she said in her most professional voice, "There's someone here to see you, Dr. Bailey. He doesn't have an appointment, but I believe you'll want to see him anyway."

Harriet felt an immediate uptick in her pulse. Will! She glanced down at the sapphire ring on her finger. Even though they were now engaged and spent a great deal of time together, she still admitted, if only to herself, that the mere mention of him caused her heart to flutter.

However, her excitement became confusion when Polly lowered her voice to a whisper. "The young gentleman comes bearing a gift and insists on giving it to you personally."

Young gentleman? Polly wouldn't describe Will that way. Arching an eyebrow, Harriet rose from her chair. "Who is it?"

With a chuckle, Polly replied, "Randy Danby." She stepped aside to allow the eleven-year-old neighbor boy to enter.

Harriet greeted him warmly. "Hi, Randy. What have you been up to this fine Thursday morning? Are you enjoying your summer holidays?"

As usual, Randy's dark hair was tousled. He wore a forest-green T-shirt and denim shorts and sported a bandage on one skinned knee. School was out for the summer, and it was clear that the boy had been spending a lot of time outdoors. He was brown as a nut, and the freckles across his nose and cheeks seemed more pronounced. His mother, Doreen, often called Randy and his four siblings her young hooligans, but she loved her children fiercely.

"Nothing much." Randy shrugged his thin shoulders. "Been riding my bike mostly, running errands for Mum and Dad, and helping around the farm as usual." He looked down at what appeared to be a pile of white tissue paper in his hands. Thrusting the bundle toward Harriet, he said, "I brought you something. I hope you like it." He ducked his head, suddenly bashful.

Polly's gaze met Harriet's, the twinkle in her friend's eyes more pronounced.

"How sweet of you," Harriet said, accepting the makeshift package. "What's the occasion? It's not my birthday or Christmas or anything."

Randy stared down at his sandal-clad feet. "I saw this figurine and thought you might like to have it. You like dogs a lot, don't you?" He regarded her with a hopeful expression.

"Indeed I do," Harriet assured him as she tugged at the parcel, which was taped with more haste than skill. "I like dogs very much. Why, this appears to be a King Charles spaniel. That's one of my favorite breeds. How did you know?"

"She always says that," Polly murmured, giving Randy a wink. "All dogs are her favorite breed."

A slow flush spread beneath Randy's freckles. "Well, I just thought you'd like it," he muttered, embarrassed. "It being a dog and kind of cute and everything."

"I do like it. Very much," Harriet assured him. She studied the brown and white porcelain figurine. It was whimsical and, in some ways, rather primitive. There was a small hole in the base, along with what appeared to be a dab of red paint. She saw no writing or markings of any kind. Could it be antique porcelain? Or simply a reproduction? She couldn't be sure. Somehow, the little dog seemed vaguely familiar. Perhaps she'd seen similar figurines at various shops in town.

"Thank you, Randy. It's adorable." Harriet gave him a bright smile. "Where did you get it?"

The boy's shoulders stiffened as he shoved his hands into the front pockets of his shorts. His flush deepened. "I found it…around. Thought you'd like it, that's all. Must be off now. Cheerio." He dashed out the clinic door like a frightened rabbit before Harriet could press the matter further.

Polly laughed as she leaned against the doorjamb, her arms folded across her chest. "You've fully cemented your position in this town, Harriet, and no mistake."

Harriet grinned at her in return. "I'm glad to hear it. He's a good kid." She walked to the waiting room and peered through the window at Randy, who was already making his getaway on his bike. "Does this look valuable to you? It might be an antique. I hope he didn't swipe it from his family's attic or anything. He seemed reluctant to tell me where he found it." She passed the figurine to Polly. "I have a feeling I recognize it somehow, but I can't place it. Do you think it belongs to Doreen? Could Randy have taken it from their house without telling her?"

"Couldn't say," Polly admitted. "But now that you've mentioned it, it does seem familiar. I must've seen others like it somewhere or other. Can't remember where." Polly handed it back to her. "You're right. It does look old."

"I'd better put it someplace safe," Harriet said. "If it does belong to Doreen, she'll want it returned in good condition. I'd hate to get Randy in trouble with his parents, but I really can't accept this if he took it without permission."

Glancing through the front window, Polly said, "There's Celia Beem with her dog, Scarlett. Right on time. The Beems are the ones who renovated the old Quill and Scroll Inn, down by the seashore. They're new in town, but they've been making friends quickly by purchasing and hiring locally."

"That's good to know, and I appreciate their commitment to feeding into the local economy. I'll see her in a moment." Harriet hurried to the kitchen, where she carefully rewrapped the porcelain dog in the tissue paper and tucked it away in a deep drawer. She'd investigate the matter later when she could have a private word with Doreen.

Randy had found the figurine, or so he'd said. But where? In his parents' attic? In someone's trash pile? Somehow, Hariet would have to convince her friend and neighbor not to be too angry with the boy, if indeed he'd taken the whimsical ornament without permission.

Harriet returned to the office to greet her newest patient—a lovely Irish setter. The dog's thirtysomething owner was petite, with strawberry-blond hair and tired blue eyes. She was rather pale, perhaps worried about the health of her pet. Still, she greeted Harriet with a shy smile. Scarlett was equally friendly, wagging her tail and fixing lively brown eyes on Harriet with interest.

"Come in and let me have a look at this gorgeous girl," Harriet said as she stroked the dog's velvety ears. "You told my receptionist that Scarlett is having skin problems?"

"Yes, and I'm at my wit's end with it," Mrs. Beem said, leading her dog into the exam room.

With Harriet's guidance, the dog bounded onto the metal table.

Mrs. Beem added, "I've changed her food and her shampoo, in case she's developed an allergy. I've also been careful to keep her bed clean. Nothing seems to help."

She told Harriet about Scarlett's paw chewing, watery eyes, sneezing, and excessive scratching while Harriet carefully examined the dog's skin.

"Based on the symptoms you're describing, I believe Scarlett has atopic dermatitis," Harriet said. "It's a chronic inflammatory skin disease associated with allergies, one of the more common in dogs."

"But what's causing it?" Mrs. Beem asked. "Is it her food? I've already tried so many brands."

"Possibly," Harriet said. "But food allergies in dogs can be tricky to identify. Has she been having gastrointestinal issues too?"

Mrs. Beem shook her head.

"That's good," Harriet told her. "Still, let's start with assuming it is a food allergy. Believe it or not, the most common symptoms of food allergies in dogs usually show up as reactions in their skin." She went on to prescribe a regimen of pills that would inhibit the inflammation and then administered the first dose. "She'll probably drink more water, but this medication should help clear up her skin, along with the modified diet."

"Thank goodness," Mrs. Beem said.

Harriet wrote everything down, from the medication dosage and schedule to the food changes she recommended and handed the sheet to Mrs. Beem. "Let me know if this doesn't help within a couple weeks, and we'll explore next steps."

"Thank you, Doctor," the woman said. "You've been so helpful. I hate to see my Scarlett in such discomfort."

"She's a beautiful animal," Harriet replied. Scarlett was a perfect example of the breed with her flashy mahogany coat, long sinewy legs, and sweet temper. Harriet stroked the dog's neck. "And you know you're a beauty, don't you, girl? We'll have you back in the pink of health before you know it." She smiled at the dog's owner. "Don't worry, Mrs. Beem. She's going to be fine."

"Please call me Celia," she replied. "All my friends do. I hope you will too."

"Then you must call me Harriet," Harriet said with a smile. "I can tell you've been worried about Scarlett, and anyone who loves animals as much as you love yours is automatically a friend of mine."

"I've not been sleeping well," Celia admitted. "But it's not Scarlett that's keeping me awake at night. It's the inn."

"Polly told me that you and your husband have renovated the old Quill and Scroll," Harriet said. "It's not easy starting a new business, or even taking over someone else's. This used to be my grandfather's veterinary practice. He built a solid practice, but it took a while for me to convince his customers they could trust me." She coaxed Scarlett off the table and opened the door, calling to Polly to come in with a treat for the dog.

Celia heaved a sigh. "It hasn't been easy. At first it sounded like so much fun. My husband, Freddie, and I love the location, and the inn is so quaint and historic. I truly enjoyed redecorating and planning menus, purchasing new towels and bed linens, picking out curtains, and modernizing the kitchen." Her mouth pinched at the corners. "But not everything has been enjoyable."

Overhearing this last comment as she strode through the door with a dog biscuit, Polly said, "Let me guess. Fire codes, leaky roofs, structural damage, leaking drains."

"Yes, all of that. You seem to know something about renovating old buildings."

"Those things are almost a guarantee with older buildings around here. I have a friend over in Pickering who bought an old manor house and turned it into a bed-and-breakfast," Polly explained. "It proved to be quite an ordeal before all was said and done. Drafty windows, unstable chimneys—all sorts of things like that." She offered the biscuit to Scarlett, who accepted it with a happy thump of her tail.

"I hope the community has been welcoming," Harriet said. "Sometimes it can be hard to fit in at first. I'm a relative newcomer myself. I came here from the States about a year ago. But now this is home, and I can't imagine living anywhere else."

Celia's face lit up. "I thought you sounded American. And yes, everyone has been very kind and supportive." She paused. "Well, *almost* everyone."

"Do tell," Polly insisted.

Harriet gave Polly a warning glance. Perhaps Celia didn't feel comfortable discussing the matter. Why should she take them into her confidence? After all, she barely knew them.

But Celia seemed willing to confide in them, though she did so in a low voice. "Mrs. Mackenzie hasn't been kind at all. And that's putting it mildly."

"Who is Mrs. Mackenzie?" Harriet asked.

"Nettie Mackenzie, the owner of the Pint Pot," Polly told her. "It's that old brick inn on the outskirts of town as you head toward Leeds."

Harriet had passed the place once or twice. It looked a bit ramshackle in her opinion, though it wasn't even half as old as the historic Quill and Scroll. There was a glorious purple clematis vine growing on the south side of the building that she greatly admired, but it was the only attractive thing about the place. She'd never been inside, nor did she know the owner, but she could well imagine that Nettie Mackenzie might be resentful of some new competition.

"She could be upset that she's likely to lose business to you and your husband," Harriet suggested. "She's probably afraid that her customers will start patronizing your place instead."

"That's what Freddie says. But he also says she'll have to get over her resentment. We're open for business, and we plan to stay. Besides, our prices are higher, or so we've been told. Not everyone will come to us. Mrs. Mackenzie will always have regular customers who wish to pay her more modest prices."

"Unfortunately, she offers mediocre food and hard beds," Polly said. "Don't lose sleep over that, Celia. She won't warm up to you and your husband anytime soon. Nettie would rather complain about competitors than improve her own establishment, and she acts as if she has a monopoly on hospitality. She's not fond of the owners of the White Hart either, so you're not alone." The White Hart was a well-known and popular inn that featured a great restaurant open to guests and non-guests alike.

"No, thinking about her rudeness doesn't keep me up at night," Celia assured them. "It's something else entirely." She flushed a deep shade of pink.

Harriet could tell the woman was embarrassed about something. She didn't want to pry and appear intrusive—or downright nosy, as her mother would say. But she remembered how it felt to be new in town, and she'd had her aunt to talk to. Celia didn't seem to have anyone except Freddie.

And, as usual, Harriet was curious.

Polly made the decision for her. "Won't you tell us? Maybe we can help. And we're very discreet. No need to worry about that."

Celia's flush deepened. After a moment's heavy pause, she said, "It's the weird noises in the inn, beyond what could be accounted for by an old building. I mean, we have the usual creaking and settling, but this is more than that, like rattling grates and whispering voices. Frankly, I'm scared. I'm almost embarrassed to admit it, but I think—I think the old inn is haunted."

CHAPTER TWO

Haunted?

Harriet couldn't believe what she'd just heard. Did Celia Beem truly believe her inn was haunted—as in, by ghosts? It sounded like something straight out of Dickens's *A Christmas Carol*, with spooks that moaned and groaned and rattled chains in the shadowy corridors. Surely the woman wasn't serious. Harriet didn't believe in ghosts. Not at all.

There was obviously some other explanation for what Celia had heard. And her pallor, the dark circles under her eyes, and her furrowed brow told Harriet that the situation was serious. Celia believed she was hearing something, that was certain. But what?

Polly cast Harriet a troubled sidelong glance. "I've never heard of the inn being haunted," she said gently. "I've lived here all my life, and so have my parents. Sure, there are the usual legends about pirates and smugglers who used to operate here. Ghost stories tend to go hand in hand with those, as well as with tales of Vikings. And we've got some ancient Roman ruins, so there's a lot of stories about long-gone centurions haunting the place. But that's all they are—stories."

Harriet leaned against a counter where she kept an array of medical supplies. She was familiar with what Polly was talking about. After a stash of antiquities from various time periods had been found in a lobster trap recently, she'd gotten a crash course in the history of the people who had inhabited the Yorkshire area over the centuries.

Celia lifted her chin. "I know you must think I'm crazy. But Freddie's heard the noises too. I'm not imagining things. He dismisses it all, of course. I know it's ludicrous to believe in ghosts. Perhaps there's some sort of animal making the noise. A squirrel, maybe? Or a trapped bird? I can't think of what else it might be. Unless the Clutterbuck brothers are playing tricks. The noises started about the same time they checked in. But why would they do such a thing? It's rather childish, and they don't strike me as the type to play pranks."

Celia was obviously frightened and worried, understandably so. As she chewed the inside of her bottom lip, Harriet wondered how she might help Celia. If the source was an animal in the wall, that was right up her alley.

"Would you describe the noises for me?" she asked. Pushing a swivel stool toward Celia, she motioned for her to have a seat.

Polly rolled in her desk chair from the outer office, apparently prepared to sit and listen too. Scarlett settled on the floor to grab a quick nap.

Harriet remained standing, leaning against the counter with her hands thrust into her pockets. Historic ghosts aside, she was intrigued. She could smell a mystery a mile off, and she was certainly getting a whiff of one now.

Celia sat with her hands clasped in her lap. "Sometimes I hear what sounds like whispering voices in the parlor, but there's no one in the room with me. Other times there are sudden loud noises. Several nights ago, the fireplace grate in the parlor gave a great jump. I thought the whole fireplace was going to fall through the floor, chimney and all. The knickknacks on the mantel even rattled and rocked."

"Sounds like the building is still settling," Polly suggested.

With a wry smile, Celia replied, "I would agree with you, but I've never heard of a house whispering while it settles. Have you?"

Celia had a point. "Did you check out the chimney?" Harriet asked, trying to pursue every logical possibility. "Maybe some loose bricks are falling, or the chimney is shifting."

Celia nodded. "Freddie even got down on his hands and knees to look up the flue. He used a torch but didn't see anything out of the ordinary. Not even a bird's nest. No loose bricks either. He ended up with nothing but soot in his hair and on his shirt."

"Perhaps something collapsed in the cellar." Polly seemed full of possibilities. "That might cause the grate to rattle."

Celia shrugged. "We explored the cellar too. The three stone walls are intact, as is the one that's made of stone and wood. Nothing appeared amiss. No toppled barrels or crates. No fallen bricks."

Watching Scarlett doze on the floor, Harriet had a thought. "What about Scarlett? Has she been with you when you heard the noises? If she has, how does she react? I would think she'd bark if there was an intruder around."

"Sometimes she barks incessantly when I can't hear a thing." Celia leaned forward to rest her elbows on her knees. "I've seen her go into the parlor and growl at an old storage bench we have in there. It freaks me out." In a lower tone, she added, "They say dogs and other animals are sensitive, you know, to ghosts and things like that."

Harriet dismissed this with a wave of her hand. Dogs were sensitive to all kinds of sounds and smells that humans couldn't detect. "Did you have a building inspector come look around before you purchased the place?" she asked.

"Of course." Celia sounded slightly indignant. "We wouldn't have made an offer on the inn without a thorough inspection. Nor would the bank have given us a mortgage. The inspection included the foundation, the cellar, the roof, and everything else. The inspector assured us the foundation was solid and the chimneys were sturdy."

"It wouldn't hurt to get a second opinion though, right?" Harriet gave her a searching glance. "A large bird could have tumbled down the chimney and dislodged something."

Celia chuckled. "It must have been the size of a pterodactyl to have dislodged something that would result in that amount of noise. I know the two of you are just trying to ease my mind. And I appreciate it. You're very kind. Freddie thinks that maybe someone is trying to scare us out of business. If so, they'd better think again. We're determined to make a go of this venture. Nothing will scare us into leaving the inn."

"Glad to hear it. Sounds as if you've been tossing around a few possibilities other than being haunted by ghosts," Harriet said.

"We have." Celia pursed her lips. "I hate to make unsubstantiated accusations, but maybe Freddie's right, and Nettie Mackenzie is playing some sort of prank. I'm sure she hopes we'll pull up stakes and leave town."

"But is she the sort of person who would break into your inn to make spooky noises in hopes of driving you away? That seems like such a childish thing to do." Harriet glanced from Celia to Polly. "Polly, you know a bit about her. Is she likely to do something so silly and possibly illegal?"

"I couldn't say for sure," Polly said. "We don't run in the same social circles, and she's closer to my mum's age than mine. I suppose I could ask Van. He might know something. I mean, if she's been in trouble with the police before, he'd know about that, right?"

Harriet considered. Yes, Detective Constable Van Worthington would know something about the innkeeper if she had a criminal record. If she didn't, he still might be able to find out something. Perhaps she'd been involved in a lawsuit or something like that.

Harriet hadn't seen the young man for a while. He'd been busy at work and spending a lot of time with Polly. The two lovebirds seemed happy as clams. Harriet almost chuckled, amused by her own mixed metaphor.

Celia cleared her throat, interrupting Harriet's reverie. "But don't you see? It's more than the grate rattling. I mentioned the whispery voices, didn't I? And the laughter? I was in the parlor dusting one day, and I heard something. It was faint, but it was unmistakably someone laughing. That rules out squirrels and birds. We had no registered guests at the time except for the Clutterbuck brothers, and they were out on the beach watching shorebirds. At least, that's what they said they were planning to do when they left the inn that morning."

Scarlett stirred, and Polly leaned over to rub her ears until she settled again. "You should have Harriet come look around," she told

Celia. "She's a regular sleuth, as sharp as any you'd like to meet. When's she's not doctoring the creatures in the county, she's solving mysteries."

Celia turned to Harriet with a piercing stare. "Really?"

Harriet shook her head. It was true she had a knack for solving mysteries, and there was obviously something mysterious going on at the Quill and Scroll. However, she could hardly see herself crawling around in a dank cellar, searching for secret passageways that might be haunted by laughing phantoms, or malicious lady innkeepers rattling the fireplace grate.

"I'm sure there must be a logical explanation," she insisted. "The wind whistling through old window frames can cause all sorts of unsettling sounds that might resemble whispering or even some sort of low-pitched laughter."

"Would you come, Harriet?" Celia pleaded. "Maybe Saturday afternoon? We'd pay for your time. Just poke around and tell us what you think might be going on. Please say you will."

After a brief pause, Harriet agreed, though she staunchly refused the offer of payment. She'd go to satisfy her own curiosity, if nothing else. Besides, she'd never been inside the place. It would be nice to see what the Beems had done with the old inn. She liked historic buildings—the older the better. "I can stop by on Saturday afternoon, if no emergencies pop up. It's certainly odd what's going on, and I'm intrigued. But I still think you should call in someone else to inspect your foundation and your roof. A second opinion would be reassuring."

Celia rose from the stool. Her eyes seemed brighter, her demeanor more relaxed than when she'd arrived. Scarlett scrambled to her feet. "Thank you, Harriet. I appreciate this more than I can say. Freddie will too when I tell him. Truly." She gripped Scarlett's leash. "Now, if you can recommend a doctor who might prescribe something so I can get a good night's sleep, I'll be on my way. I've taken up enough of your time already."

With a broad smile, Harriet replied, "I can indeed recommend someone. Dr. Genevieve Garrett has an office right next door. Her receptionist can make an appointment for you. Dr. Garrett is my aunt."

"And a fine physician," Polly chimed in.

With Celia and Scarlett on their way, Polly informed Harriet that there were no more scheduled appointments for the day. "Do you mind if I cut out early?" she asked. "I promised Mum I'd take her to the bank and the general store."

Harriet readily agreed. Polly and her mother shared a vehicle. Sometimes Polly rode her bicycle to work. At other times, her mother dropped her off and picked her up after work. That morning, Polly had dropped off her mother and driven herself to work. Anyone calling the office after closing would be rerouted to Harriet's cell phone, so there was no need for Polly to sit at the desk twiddling her thumbs.

Besides, Harriet could use the opportunity to catch up on some paperwork and make a few follow-up calls. She wanted to schedule another visit for that chameleon with the broken front leg to make sure he had healed properly.

As Polly retrieved her purse from the bottom drawer of the reception desk, she glanced out the window. "My, aren't you popular today? Looks like you have another gentleman caller bearing gifts."

"Who is it this time?" Harriet asked, puzzled.

"Your knight in shining armor."

Harriet stepped up to peer over Polly's shoulder. Pastor Will Knight strolled across the parking area, carrying a shoebox. Will, her fiancé. He was indeed her knight in shining armor. Harriet's lips curled into a soft smile as she recalled how he'd dropped to one knee when he'd proposed to her. It had been picture-perfect, on the seashore with an early sunset coloring the sky.

"I wonder what's in the shoebox." She suspected he wasn't bringing her a pair of shoes.

"So do I, but I can't keep Mum waiting." Polly pushed the door open, giving the pastor a cheerful greeting as they passed each other in the doorway.

Will responded in kind before flashing a warm smile in Harriet's direction. "Good afternoon, Harriet. Ah, hello, Charlie," he added as the office cat slipped past him through the door.

Harriet had inherited Charlie along with her grandfather's home and business. The calico was the latest in a long line of office cats Harold Bailey had dubbed "Charlie" regardless of gender so that he had one less thing to remember. Though Charlie's coat was patchy, due to scars left by the trash bin fire she'd been rescued from as a kitten, Harriet had yet to meet a sweeter or cleverer cat.

"Where's Maxwell?" Will asked, referring to the clinic dog, a long-haired dachshund Harriet's grandfather had taken in after a car accident had left his back half paralyzed. He scampered around quite well in his wheeled prosthesis.

Harriet stepped forward to press a kiss on Will's smooth cheek. "Snoozing somewhere. That dog never misses an afternoon nap if he can help it." She nodded toward the shoebox, which she could now see had several holes poked in the top. "And what do we have here?"

His expression became more somber as he replied, "You're probably the only woman I know who might be interested or even pleased by this. You'd better see for yourself."

Harriet took the box from his hands and lifted the lid. When she recognized the contents, she gasped.

CHAPTER THREE

White Church Bay
June 1941

"Is everything all right, Flory?"

Florence Birtwhistle turned her gaze away from the World War I monument and found herself face-to-face with Miss Edith Dingle. The short, sturdy, middle-aged woman with a wealth of mouse-brown hair tucked under a worn felt hat was a pillar of the community. She was also the indefatigable president of the local chapter of the Women's Institute. Miss Dingle knew everybody, and everybody knew Miss Dingle. They respected her too. She had a friendly, no-nonsense manner. Flory admired her greatly.

"I'm just woolgathering, Miss Dingle," she replied with a smile, adjusting the bonnet of her baby daughter's pram. It was a real pram too, not one of those cheap "boxes on wheels" without padding or springs that had been recently produced to save valuable resources for the war effort.

"About Donald perhaps?" Edith's smile was soft and sympathetic.

Flory nodded. Her husband and so many other men from the village were away at war. Heaven only knew where exactly. France, probably. That's what he'd told her before shipping out. She sent up another silent prayer for his safety, glancing again at the war memorial with the names of men who'd died in the previous war. The War to End All Wars, they'd called it. Someone had been overly optimistic.

Familiar surnames ran over the memorial—Jenkins, Birtwhistle, O'Malley, Danby, Bennett, Richardson, Worthington, and so many more. Scarcely a family in the village had been untouched by the heartbreak of war. The English lost a million lives in that war, which meant that everyone had lost someone—a husband, brother, fiancé, cousin, a father. The monument stood as a grim reminder.

Edith leaned over the pram. "Such a precious little lamb. How old is Jane now?"

Flory felt grateful for the distraction. War and loss were always too prevalent on her mind. "Almost six months," she replied. She sent up another prayer of thanksgiving that Jane was too young to know what was going on. She'd heard some of the other mothers fretting about their youngsters' endless questions about where their fathers had gone, when they would be coming back, and why the Germans were dropping bombs. Flory wanted to protect Jane's innocence for as long as possible. How she hoped the war would end before her girl was old enough to ask questions of her own.

"I saw the Home Guard out this morning on the beach with more rolls of barbed wire," Edith said. "I suppose your father is out there with them?"

Flory turned her head in that direction. Yes, her father, John Woodley, was on the beach with the rest of the men in the Home Guard. They patrolled the shore regularly. The summer sun glistened on the sea in the distance like sparkling diamonds. Peaceful. Or so it appeared. But were German U-boats even now prowling the coast, preparing for an invasion as her father feared? If so, Flory didn't suppose the barbed wire would stop the invaders for long, but at least it would slow them down some.

"Your father is a good man," Edith said. "Salt of the earth."

"Yes." Flory didn't know what else to say. Her dad was a good man, loyal to king and country. John Woodley had fought in that first war. He knew things about fighting the Germans. They'd been called Huns back in the day, he'd told her. The new generation was called Nazis.

Flory and her baby daughter lived with her father still. Even after her marriage to Donald Birtwhistle, they'd made their home with her parents. Her dad was a stonemason. Not much call now for building new walls and homes, but there was always a need for repairing existing ones. And tombstones. Her father had far too many orders for those these days. Donald had been learning the trade before he was called up.

Mrs. Mavis White strode briskly toward them, a market basket over one arm. "Good morning, Miss Dingle, Flory." She had a soft, rather husky voice. Tall and slender, the woman appeared so youthful that one would hardly guess that she was the mother of three rambunctious boys and a pert five-year-old girl. "You might drop in on the fishmonger," she suggested to Flory. "He has quite a fine selection this morning."

"Oh, thank you. I'll do that," Flory replied. As a nursing mother, she was entitled to larger rations than most. She was glad her hardworking father benefited as well.

"Mavis, I wanted to tell you that your Peggy made a fine flower girl in Sharon Merritt's wedding," Edith said. "Pretty as a picture, she was. Almost as pretty as the bride."

Mavis beamed. "Thank you, Miss Dingle. The little love did look a treat, didn't she? And so pleased she was to have a new dress—even if it was only one made over from her aunt's pink nightie."

Flory's lips twitched. Little Peggy White was pretty, it was true. But Sharon Merritt had been an exceptionally lovely bride. She'd walked down the aisle in her mother's wedding gown, tailored to her own tastes. The poor girl, like so many other wartime brides, had worn her bedroom slippers down the aisle too. Shoes were rationed, and no one in the village had a suitable pair in Sharon's size. What else could one do? Yet the joy and love on her face had made her as stunning as any princess.

"Now, Miss Dingle, you mustn't let my Peggy hear your praise. You'll give the child a big head. Besides, my dear mother—God rest her soul—always used to say, 'Pretty is as pretty does.'"

Edith said, "I remember your mother. An exceptional woman. As was yours, Flory. They are sorely missed in our community. Both would have been pleased to see the Merritt girl wed to such a fine man. It's a shame young Ratchford had to leave for France so soon. This war is so awful." She shook her head, which set the artificial daisy on her hat to swaying. "At least the couple had a decent wedding breakfast."

"The cake was delicious." Flory had a sweet tooth and didn't care who knew it. All the Merritts' neighbors and relatives had saved rations so there would be enough butter, sugar, and eggs to make a decent wedding cake. Without icing, of course. It was now illegal to frost a cake, according to the Ministry of Food. Instead, Sharon's mother had arranged a lovely display of pink and red rosebuds on the top, which made the cake look quite festive.

"At least flowers aren't rationed," Mavis added, leaning over the pram to smile at Jane, who giggled and cooed.

True, there had been plenty of flowers. Perhaps that was why so many brides married in June. There was always an abundance of flowers for the church and the dining tables set out for the occasion.

Lowering her voice, Mavis observed, "I see the Home Guard is busy on the beach again this morning."

"Yes, my father is with them," Flory told her.

"Has there been news? Any updates about the possible invasion? What is your father's opinion?" Mavis pressed. "Does he think the Nazis will come by sea, or by air?"

Flory swallowed hard. She hated to think about a possible invasion, but it was all anyone ever talked about anymore. Her father seldom spoke frankly of such things. He feared additional stress would make her incapable of nursing Jane. Too many new mothers, exhausted and fearful, already faced that difficulty.

Edith spoke up. "I suspect they'll drop from the sky over London first. Their pilots have had enough practice during the Blitz, haven't they?" She gave an indignant huff. "I feel certain they could fly over the Channel blindfolded by now."

The Blitz. Flory shuddered at the mere mention of the word. The nonstop bombing of London and other major cities had taken place nightly for nearly nine months. The deaths and injuries and destruction nearly broke her heart—but not her spirit.

"Any word from Donald?" Edith asked, changing the subject with a smile.

"Nothing this week or last," Flory said. Her husband wasn't much of a letter writer at the best of times. And this was not the best of times, with mail delivery so unpredictable.

Edith patted her arm. "We'll be seeing you at the next WI meeting, won't we, Flory? And you too, Mavis? We're sharing a recipe for tomato chutney, and a councilman will be there to explain about collecting bones for the munition factories."

"Wouldn't miss it for the world," Mavis chirped.

Flory added, "I'll be there too." She wasn't much interested in a chutney recipe, because she loved the recipe she'd gotten from her mother, but she was interested in learning about the saving of chicken, ham, and rabbit bones. What about fish bones? Should she be saving those too? These days they were always salvaging something—metal, paper, cloth, and now bones. All for the war effort, of course.

"We must all do our part," Edith went on, as if reading Flory's thoughts. "And for fun, I believe there will be a beetle drive."

A beetle drive was a fundraiser based on a popular parlor game. It was traditionally played with pen, paper, and a gaming die. Players would roll the die and collect various parts of a hypothetical beetle, such as the body, the head, and the wings, which they'd track on the paper by drawing the parts corresponding to the die rolls they'd gotten. The first person to assemble a whole beetle was the winner.

For the fundraiser, attendees would buy tickets. Players were split into groups that shared a single die. Every time a player won, the groups would shuffle. Each beetle part collected gave that player a point, and whoever had the most points after the agreed-upon number of games won the whole game and a donated grand prize.

Mavis grinned. "Those are such fun. But I wouldn't miss a WI meeting even if we didn't have beetle drives and other games. I relish those get-togethers more than I can say. I enjoy a good chin-wag with other women from time to time. It breaks up the monotony of knitting at home and canning preserves. Besides, it's a good opportunity to swap recipes."

Edith gave her a nod of approval. "I enjoy them myself. There are so many ways we can help the war effort, and the

Women's Institute meetings help train us to do so. Think of it. Women across the country are holding meetings just like ours. Those Nazis haven't beaten us yet." She straightened her shoulders. "I must get on. And Flory, you must stop in at the fishmonger. Maybe you can get a nice piece of mackerel or cod for supper."

"Yes, I'll do that. See you both at the WI meeting," Flory promised.

Pushing the pram, she made her way to the fishmonger, where she produced her ration book and purchased a piece of cod and a plaice fillet, knowing how her father enjoyed both.

Afterward, she stopped briefly at the stationer's store to buy a journal, one with lined pages and a simple canvas cover, although she did gaze longingly at the tooled leather covers on the more expensive ones. Not too many of those nowadays, with both paper and leather being in short supply. Inspired by a recent lecture at the WI, Flory had made up her mind to keep a diary of her daily life during the war. When he returned home—when, not if—Donald might be interested in how she had kept the home fires burning. So might Jane, one day.

When Flory took her selection to the counter, she noticed a jar of black-and-white humbugs near the register.

Mr. Hocking, red-faced, balding, and good-natured, caught the interested gleam in her eye. With a wink, he said, "Mrs. Birtwhistle, may I offer you a piece of candy? You and your babe are the prettiest customers to brighten my store this fine summer day. And to my mind, you should be rewarded."

Flory didn't hold back a laugh. Did everyone know about her sweet tooth? She was particularly fond of the peppermint-flavored confection, and sweets were getting harder and harder to come by. "Thank you, Mr. Hocking. That's most generous of you." She helped herself to a humbug and popped it into her mouth.

After paying for her purchase, Flory tucked the new journal into the pram at Jane's feet and strode briskly through the village. Back at the little cottage she called home, she put away her purchases and peeled potatoes to fry with the fish later when her father returned home for his meal. She glanced at the lamb shank she was saving for tomorrow's stew and thought again of bones. She frowned. They'd been told to start saving bones for the munitions factories. But how could she keep the old bones from stinking up the kitchen? And what on earth did the factories want with bones anyway?

CHAPTER FOUR

"I found the poor little creature on the floor of the belfry," Will said, shoving his hands into the front pockets of his black trousers. "He's not looking too good in my opinion. I thought I'd better bring him to you. I don't know anything about nursing bats."

Harriet held her breath as she peered at the small bat wrapped in a worn dish towel. She reached for a face mask and a pair of disposable gloves. It was the closest she'd ever been to a bat. In all her years of training and treating animals as a veterinarian, she'd never actually examined one.

Of course, she knew several basic facts. Bats were the only flying mammal—the flying squirrel could glide, but that wasn't the same—and they swooped around at dusk, eating insects. She'd read that bats played a vital role in the world's ecosystems. However, on the downside, they could also quickly form a roost in the top of various buildings, posing health risks like rabies and parasites.

Leaning over the bat, Harriet noted the fur on its torso. The creature was dark brown in color, with a short snout and large ears. The scalloped edging at the bottom of its wings reminded her a bit of an old-fashioned umbrella. Its skin was leathery and rubbery.

She peered closer. "Oh dear," she murmured. "It's barely breathing. To tell the truth, I'm not sure how to help it." Was it diseased or injured?

Perhaps it was dehydrated or even starving. Her mind raced with possibilities. "You didn't touch it with your bare hands, did you, Will?"

"No, I used the tea towel to pick him up off the floor. The only container at hand was that old shoebox. Why, hello, Maxwell." Will bent down to stroke the dog, who'd scampered into the room at the sound of Will's voice. Maxwell lifted his head for a chin rub, and Will readily obliged.

"That's good. Bats can carry diseases that affect humans and other animals," she told him.

His eyes widened in alarm. "I had no idea. Now I'm sorry I brought it in, Harriet. You could become infected with something, and if you did, I'd never forgive myself. Please be careful. Take all the necessary precautions."

Harriet pointed at her mask then wiggled the fingers of her gloved hands. "Don't worry. I'll be all right." At least, she hoped so. She made a mental note to spend some time doing research on bats in the UK. If there were bats in the neighborhood—and obviously there were—she needed to learn more about them. "However, you and Maxwell aren't wearing protective gear. How would you feel about taking him out into the garden for a run?"

"Are you sure? I hate to leave you alone in a dangerous situation I caused."

She loved how considerate he was. "Quite sure. Polly has a ball for him on her desk. He loves chasing it, and he usually wakes up from his afternoon nap full of energy."

Reluctantly, Will agreed.

With Will and Maxwell out of the room, Harriet continued her examination. She gave the bat a few drops of water with an eye dropper and placed it along with the dish towel in an empty birdcage she kept for some of her more exotic boarders.

After removing her mask and gloves and dropping them in a sanitary container for waste materials, she carried the cage out to the garden. "I think this little guy just needs food and water. I don't really know for sure. I'm taking it to the barn for safekeeping. I haven't had any experience dealing with bats. The poor thing is rather small, so it might even be a pup that got separated from its mother."

Will followed her to the barn. "What are you going to do with it?"

"Hope the warm weather, relative darkness, and quiet in the barn help it start to recover," Harriet replied. "Beyond that, I'm not sure yet. Bats are a protected species here in the UK, according to my grandfather's veterinary science journals. Unfortunately, I didn't read those sections about treatment as thoroughly as I should have." She considered the problem. "I'll call Dr. Witty."

Dr. Gavin Witty had been a colleague of her grandfather, and he was also one of several area vets who'd immediately taken Harriet under his wing. The tall, red-haired veterinarian would know exactly what to do. He'd been quite helpful in the past, and she valued his insight.

"Protected? Why? Are they endangered or something?" Will asked.

"I believe their numbers have been greatly reduced," Harriet said. "Loss of habitat and the decline of insect populations, I guess. I hope I can save the poor little thing." After finding a safe place for the birdcage, she said, "Let's go wash our hands. We can't be too careful."

"Yes, Doctor," Will said, trailing her back to the clinic.

Harriet smiled at him then sobered again. "I wonder how a little bat pup made its way into the belfry all by itself. Did you see any others? They aren't solitary creatures. Where there's one, there are usually more."

"Please don't tell me that." Will shuddered as he scrubbed his hands with soap at the sink. "No, I didn't see any others. But to be honest, I didn't look very hard. I mean, I was startled when I discovered that one. I went up there to check the floorboards to make sure they're still solid and to see if the bell ropes need to be replaced. As I said, the bat seemed to be having difficulty breathing, so I thought I should bring it here right away."

Harriet shrugged. "No worries. We can check into it later."

"I don't like the idea of bats anywhere in the church," Will said, drying his hands. "I've always heard the phrase 'bats in the belfry' but never considered we might have them in ours. It would be easy enough for them to get in. I dread thinking about bats chewing on the wiring or whatever it is they do." He made a face. "Perhaps I should call someone to remove them. If there is a colony, as you suggest, this little guy and his one hundred cousins need to be taken away."

Harriet gazed up into his face with a rueful smile. "You can't call a pest-removal person. Remember, the bats are protected by law. They can't be exterminated—especially during the season when baby bats are born. The pups need to be protected. They might not be able to be relocated until after they're grown. I don't know. I'll ask Dr. Witty."

"But who'll protect the church from the bats?" Will protested. "I can't have them swooping down on my parishioners during services or compromising the rafters."

Harriet understood his concern. She could almost imagine the ruckus that would cause during a Sunday morning service—the shrieks and shouts as a colony of bats darted about the sanctuary, plunging here and there among the congregation, settling on the back of a pew or on the shoulder of an unsuspecting parishioner.

Then Will added, "I don't want bats tangling in the hair of our wedding guests either."

She agreed wholeheartedly. "I'm pretty sure bats don't chew insulation or wiring and drywall or anything. And I seriously doubt they'll come swooping down on us during a worship service. They tend to be shy creatures. Besides, how would they get from the belfry into the sanctuary? I promise I'll call Dr. Witty. As I said, he'll know what to do not only with our patient but also about checking for bat roosts in the church and what to do if we find one."

"You're right. I don't have enough information to worry yet," Will said.

Harriet checked the time. "Have you had tea, Will? I can put the kettle on and make a few sandwiches. I have a jar of that spicy mustard you like. And I've got part of an iced lemon loaf that Aunt Jinny made the other day."

"Sounds delightful. Lead the way."

Harriet made her way to the kitchen with Will, Maxwell, and Charlie on her heels. Will put the kettle on and gathered the other necessities for tea.

As Harriet assembled the bread, meat, and cheese for the sandwiches, her thoughts about bats merged with possible causes of Celia Beem's problem at the inn. She mused aloud, "I wonder how noisy bats are? I can imagine them making a sort of whispery sound or rustling as they move their wings about. But what about their vocalizations? Perhaps the Beems have bat problems."

"The Beems? Do you mean that nice young couple who are renovating the Quill and Scroll?" Will retrieved cups and saucers from the cabinet. "I didn't know they were having any problems. Nothing serious, I hope."

"We're not sure yet. Celia brought her Irish setter in today. She mentioned that they've heard some strange noises in the parlor." Harriet gave Will a summary of her earlier conversation with Celia and the woman's concern that the inn might be haunted. "I didn't think of it at the time, but maybe they have a bat infestation. A large roost could be causing the trouble." That might explain the whispering sounds if not the rattle of the old grate.

Still, one couldn't be sure until another inspection was done on the property. Harriet hoped Celia would take that suggestion seriously. The first building inspector may have overlooked something.

As they enjoyed the light meal, Harriet watched Will consume his food with gusto. Her heart felt a rush of love for this man, the man she intended to spend the rest of her life with. They both wanted a big wedding, and Harriet had discovered that planning one would require considerable time and effort from both of them. But for now she pondered the joy of all the quiet, simple meals they would share together in the future. It warmed her heart and filled her with unspeakable joy. How blessed she was.

As soon as they'd finished eating, Will cleared the table and Harriet reached for her cell phone. Perusing her list of contacts, she tapped Dr. Gavin Witty's name with a silent apology for asking him to work after hours. Like her, he was always on call and had gotten used to being summoned at all hours of the day and night. Interruptions were a professional hazard. She'd been warned back at the university what it would be like. Truth be told, she didn't really mind. An animal's health was always more important to her than her own time. She hoped Gavin felt the same way.

He answered on the first ring. "Hello, Harriet. How are you?"

She got right to the point. "A bit stumped and hoping you can help, Gavin. What can you tell me about nursing a bat, possibly a baby, back to health? I'm putting you on speaker. Pastor Will Knight is here with me. He found the bat in the church and brought it to me."

"Hi, Dr. Witty," Will chimed in.

"Evening, Pastor. You found a single bat?" the man asked. "Where exactly was it?"

Harriet and Will filled him in on all the information they had and answered his questions as well as they could.

"I think I understand. Do you have a pencil or a pen handy?" Gavin asked. "As Harriet knows, dealing with a protected species can be tricky. I'm going to give you the address and phone number of the Bat Conservation Trust. You'll need to get in touch with them. They'll explain all the necessary procedures."

He went on to talk about the mission of the trust—to ensure that all bat species in the UK were protected, along with their breeding and resting sites. Harriet scribbled notes on the notepad she kept on the kitchen counter near the toaster. Will listened to the conversation with a concerned expression.

As Gavin explained the legalities involved, Harriet felt mildly dismayed. Dealing with a bat was proving to be more complicated than she'd imagined. She was also concerned with how little Gavin said she would be able to help the bat without official certifications. She could only do the bare minimum by providing it with food and water and keeping it in a dark, quiet area.

"Will is concerned there may be more bats somewhere in the church building," Harriet told Gavin. "Perhaps an entire colony. If we can't call a pest removal company, what can we do?"

"It's a tough situation and no mistake," Gavin said. "Especially at this time of year. June is a prime time for bats to be born. There may be a bat roost either somewhere in the church building or somewhere nearby. We also have a lot of caves in the vicinity, as you know. Bats are at their most active during the summer months, particularly young bats. They start to explore their immediate environment and can be quite curious. Unfortunately, sometimes they get lost from their roost and seek shelter in a small gap beneath a roof or fly through an open window. Since we can't remove a colony, this problem might last a while. Perhaps all through the summer months."

"Oh dear." Harriet glanced at Will again. He didn't appear too happy with that answer.

Gavin went on. "Sometimes young, inexperienced flyers will become exhausted before finding their way out. They may try to land on a wall or cling to the curtains. They might even crash-land on a piece of furniture or on the floor. I suppose that could be the case with the bat the vicar found, since he only found the one."

"So what do we do now, exactly?" Harriet pressed.

"You'll have to call the national bat helpline. Take some time to read the information on the website too. And remember, you're not permitted to disturb the roost during pup season, if indeed there is one in the belfry or somewhere else in the church building."

"Dr. Witty, is there anything we can do to prevent more bats from getting inside the church?" Will asked.

"Certainly. If the bats are confined to the belfry, they shouldn't be too much of a problem. However, you'd better look for any gaps around the pipes in the bathrooms, around the window frames, between the floor joists, and in the ceiling or skirting corners," he informed them. "But you must be careful when attempting to seal those entry points. Bats can become stuck to the sealant or poisoned by the fumes."

Harriet thanked her colleague for his help and promised she'd contact the bat trust right away. She wanted to take some time to explore the website to learn more about bats in the UK and how best to handle any future bats that might come her way. She wanted to respect the laws regarding their protection without allowing them to cause issues in the church—or in the Beems' inn, if the creatures were causing the strange noises there.

Something had to be done.

CHAPTER FIVE

White Church Bay
June 1941

"Now, how many of you good ladies here have roses in your gardens?" The woman at the podium in the pale green linen suit glanced around the room. Her iron-gray hair was cut short and slightly resembled a close-fitting helmet.

Flory raised her hand along with most of the other women. Though the government was urging everyone to tear out their shrubs and flower beds to turn them into victory gardens, she would never uproot the lovely pink floribunda roses her mother had planted so many years ago. For Flory, they were a tangible way to keep her mother's memory alive.

Many families had sacrificed their lilac bushes, delphiniums, and prize dahlias in favor of crops like cabbage, brussels sprouts, and carrots. Gone were the attractive rock gardens, lush lawns, and herbaceous borders, but few of the women present would willingly uproot their roses. Digging for victory was all well and good, but like Flory, sacrificing one's roses was going too far. Roses fed the soul just as carrots and cabbages fed the body.

"Wonderful! I'm sure you grow lovely roses here in the Bay," the woman at the podium declared.

The speaker had come from the chapter of the Women's Institute in Leeds. Miss Dingle had invited her to lecture about collecting rose hips. And while Flory didn't recall the woman's name, she certainly admired the speaker's linen suit. It looked new, not refashioned or mended like so many garments these days.

"Now, here's what you can do to help the pharmaceutical companies as they support the war effort." The woman went on to explain about collecting rose hips following the first frost. She explained that they could be turned into syrup for medicines to combat kidney stones, hypertension, respiratory illnesses, and gastrointestinal problems. "And rose hips have proven to have anti-inflammatory properties as well, which are very important for our soldiers and airmen recovering from war wounds."

"Coo," Marietta Trumble murmured in a tone of amazement. She sat next to Flory, scribbling in a small blue notebook with the stub of a well-used pencil.

Miss Muncie, one of the primary school teachers, also appeared to be taking notes on Marietta's other side. "My gran always said you can learn something new every day."

Flory smoothed her skirt over her knees, wondering if she should be taking notes. She would never remember everything shared here today. There was always so much to learn at the WI meetings, and she knew her father would pump her for all the information when she got home.

The woman at the podium went on. "I know it's only June, and you must be thinking you need not worry about collecting rose hips right now. But time flies, as they say. The first frost will be upon us before we know it. We must be prepared to harvest the rose hips then."

Realizing she'd slumped in the hard-backed chair, Flory sat up straighter and stretched her shoulders, grateful for a little time away from the baby and out of the kitchen. As usual, Dad had willingly agreed to keep an eye on Jane so Flory could attend the monthly WI meeting at the town hall. No doubt he'd taken his hoe to the cabbages now in the cool of the evening. Jane would be in her pram. After he'd weeded the garden to his satisfaction, he'd come inside, put the kettle on, and listen to the wireless.

Marietta had stopped by for Flory in her husband's milk lorry. Simon Trumble always had enough petrol rations. He had to deliver the milk, after all. He no longer made daily deliveries, however. It was now only three times a week, but people made do. Simon had not been called up for military duty, because of some health problems, much to his chagrin. Marietta was one of the lucky few who still had her husband at home. Flory didn't feel jealous, simply wistful. She wouldn't have wished a disability on Donald, not even to keep him safe at home.

On the way to the town hall, seated next to each other in the lorry, Marietta had pushed a small brown paper parcel toward Flory. "Tuck that away in your handbag for now. It's a bit of cheddar."

"Thank you so much," Flory gushed.

How blessed she was to have such a friend, who gave so freely of resources that were as precious as gold these days. Even though Flory was entitled to more rations than most, Marietta had been sharing extra milk or even a half pint of cream cheese when possible, ever since Jane was born. "Nursing mothers have to keep up their strength," Marietta reminded her often enough.

Flory was more concerned about keeping up her spirits. It was all too easy to become disheartened. She tried to stay cheerful and optimistic. Putting on her Sunday best to attend a WI meeting was one way she hoped to achieve that. Others surely felt the same. Most of the women present were attired in their summer best—some with hats, and short white gloves to hide their work-roughened hands. The room was redolent with the pleasant aromas of lilac soap and lily of the valley cologne, no doubt carefully hoarded and used only on special occasions.

Any interested woman was invited to attend, even if they weren't members of the institute. Several Women's Land Army girls were recognizable by their sunburned noses and tan, well-muscled arms. Much of Britain's food had been imported before the First World War. When that war broke out and many of the country's male agricultural workers *were called up to fight, the women had stepped up to improve food production. They had come together again for this war, volunteering to work the land to keep the nation going.*

Miss Dingle was present, of course. As president of the local chapter, she'd opened the meeting with prayer, asking God's blessing on the soldiers on the battlefields, the pilots in the air, and the seamen in peril on the waters.

The district nurse, Sister Cupit, sat on the front row, listening intently to everything.

Flory almost didn't recognize the woman out of her nurse's uniform. She served as head of the institute's finance committee and did a scrupulous job of it too.

Flory finally learned what saving bones was all about. Apparently, they could be used in factories to make glycerin for explosives, glue, fertilizer, soap, and more. Who knew? Authorities were asking that civilians save rabbit, pork, beef, and even squirrel bones.

The salvage steward of the district spoke next, explaining how the women could dry the bones at low temperatures in the oven. He then suggested storing them in a closed bin or on a shelf in the larder until they were collected. He went on to entertain them with humorous incidents of dogs and even cats pilfering supplies that had not been properly stored.

The government continued to urge everyone to reuse all the bits and bobs that normally would be tossed in the rubbish. Everything that could be recycled should be recycled. Flory supposed it was inevitable that they should save bones as well for the war effort. What next?

Swap parties and bartering had become a way of life too. Why, she'd swapped a pair of her mother's shoes, which didn't fit her, for the handbag she'd brought with her tonight.

As the women around her raised their hands to ask questions, Flory felt her shoulders relax. It was pleasant to simply sit and listen to the conversation around her without being mindful of the baby or worried about scorching something on the stove in the hot kitchen. And her hands were still for once. She needn't worry about dropping a stitch while knitting. It seemed she was always knitting these days—even on hot summer days.

The local Dorcas Society had supplied wool to be knitted into socks for the troops, so most women and girls were always knitting when not busy doing something else. Once in a while contests were held to see how many socks one could knit in a week. The winners received prizes—sometimes a box of chocolates. Flory never won, but she didn't mind. She was a slow knitter, but careful and sure. There were no lumps or bumps in the heels, and no one could have asked for a neater toe seam than hers. No poor soldier or sailor would get a blister wearing her socks.

Marietta nudged her, interrupting her reveries. "Time for tea."

Flory practically leapt to her feet. She was always hungry these days. As usual, following the lectures, the women gathered at a long table at the back of the room where the hospitality committee presented a tantalizing array of simple refreshments—dainty sandwiches with a smear of potted meat, or tomato with mayonnaise and watercress. She knew the egg salad sandwiches had been made with powdered eggs and were no doubt generously salted to mask the odd taste, but food was food. A platter of ginger biscuits and small cherry tarts attracted her attention immediately. Had they been sweetened with rationed sugar, or golden syrup?

Helping herself to a neat triangle-shaped sandwich filled with fish paste and a cucumber slice, Flory mused, "I wonder what they did with the crusts?"

"Tossed to the chickens, I'd wager," Marietta replied. "Everyone's keeping chickens now. Or used in a bread pudding maybe. That's what I do. Can't waste a thing, you know."

Yes, she knew.

As the women formed small chatty clusters, they exchanged bits of news about absent husbands and complaints about the latest ration requirements—especially the new clothing rationing. The subject of Anderson shelters came up again, and Flory wondered if she should talk her father into getting one of the do-it-yourself bomb shelters. He insisted their root cellar was protection enough if bombers flew out their way, but Flory wasn't so sure. Frankly, she even resented the gas mask, which everyone was now required to carry around along with their handbags.

And yet, there was Daphne Day, who'd dared come to the meeting without hers.

"Daphne forgot her gas mask again," Marietta hissed as though reading Flory's thoughts. "But she remembered to wear lipstick, didn't she?"

Just as Miss Dingle had suggested, a beetle drive was held following the refreshments. Mavis White won the game and a chocolate bar for her efforts. Her delight was so effusive that Flory suddenly didn't care that she'd only collected her beetle's body, head, and a single leg.

As the evening's meeting drew to an end, Miss Dingle beckoned to Flory and Marietta. "I wonder if I might ask you both to come to tea tomorrow afternoon. You're sensible young women." She glanced over her shoulder as if to see whether anyone was listening, "I have something I wish to discuss with you two, and a few others here as well."

"I can come," Marietta replied immediately.

"As can I, but I'll have to bring Jane," Flory said. "Is that all right?"

Miss Dingle waved a hand as though dismissing Flory's concerns. "Bring the wee babe, of course. We must make plans. There are important preparations to be made."

"Preparations for what?" Marietta asked.

Miss Dingle's eyes widened. "Why, the German invasion, naturally. They'll be here before the summer's end."

CHAPTER SIX

Harriet explored the Bat Conservation Trust website for a considerable amount of time. She'd just filled out the required form requesting assistance when her cell phone rang.

"Do you have plans for dinner tonight?" Aunt Jinny asked as soon as Harriet answered.

Harriet smiled. It had been three busy days since she'd last spoken with her aunt. It was good to hear her cheerful voice. "Not really, other than eating something sooner or later. I had a late lunch with Will, but he's tending to his flock this evening. He's gone to sit with Mr. Trumble so Mrs. Trumble can have dinner with her sister and then attend choir practice."

"How kind," Aunt Jinny declared. "Will is such a good shepherd for his flock. We are blessed to have him as our pastor, and I'm so thankful he'll soon be my nephew-in-law as well."

Harriet agreed. It was just like Will to offer to spend time with elderly Edward Trumble, who suffered with dementia. His wife, Yvonne, didn't dare leave her husband on his own for fear he might injure himself or wander off. Members of the church family took turns sitting with Edward so his wife could have a much-needed respite now and then.

"Would you like to walk into town and have some fish and chips?" Aunt Jinny asked. "It's a lovely evening, and I could use the fresh air and exercise. To say nothing of a catch-up with you."

"I would love to go," Harriet replied. Spending time with her aunt was one of her favorite things.

Although they lived next door to each other, both led busy lives and didn't get to spend nearly as much time together as Harriet would like. Her aunt had been instrumental in helping her adjust to life in their small Yorkshire town, to say nothing of her continuous encouragement while Harriet took over Grandad's business.

"I'll meet you in the car park in twenty minutes," Harriet promised.

"Can't wait," her aunt replied cheerily.

Harriet freshened up and put on a light jacket in case the evening temperature dropped by the time she was on her way home. She looked forward to the walk into the village. Summer evenings were long. Sometimes the sun didn't set until nine o'clock or later depending on the weather, so they didn't need to worry about walking home in the dark. It would be light enough. And it would feel good to get some fresh air and stretch her legs. She loved the feel of the sea breeze on her face, the salty tang in the air.

She fed Maxwell and Charlie, washed her hands, and then snatched up her small shoulder bag and made sure her cell phone was tucked securely in the outside pocket. She never knew when one of her animal patients might need immediate attention.

As she strode toward the car park, Harriet waved at Ida Winslow, who was just getting into her vehicle. Ida managed the art gallery on the property. On top of being a beloved vet, Harriet's grandfather had become somewhat famous for his paintings of landscapes and animals, and the gallery displayed his work for the public to enjoy.

Ida waved back, and Harriet wondered what had kept her working so late. But then, it *was* summer, and tourist season was in full swing. Many visitors stopped by the gallery to admire the paintings and buy prints. No doubt Ida had plenty to do these days.

Aunt Jinny joined her, looking comfortable in khakis and a denim blazer, and said, "I see Ida's just now leaving. Doesn't the gallery usually close at four?"

"Usually," Harriet replied. "She must have been catching up on receipts and other paperwork."

They took the cliff path toward the village in companionable silence. In the distance, sunbeams sparkled on the water. Wildflowers lined the path with a riot of color, and bees hummed gently. She experienced a warm rush of well-being and gratitude for the Lord bringing her to this place, this blessed life.

Finally, Harriet broke the pleasant quiet. "Aunt Jinny, I referred a new patient to you today. Celia Beem. Did she contact you?"

"Yes, she came into the office this afternoon to make an appointment, but Moira sent her right in. There'd been a cancellation," Aunt Jinny said. "I also got to meet her beautiful Irish setter. One of your patients, I presume."

"Scarlett, yes," Harriet said with a smile. "Celia came to you directly from a visit at the clinic for Scarlett's skin problems."

"Oh dear. Is everything all right?" Aunt Jinny asked.

"It should be in time," Harriet reassured her. "Did Celia happen to mention a problem at the inn?"

Aunt Jinny frowned. "What sort of problem?"

"A spooky one." Harriet gave a mock shudder.

"Spooky?" Aunt Jinny echoed. "As in ghosts?"

"Celia suggested that, but of course, there's no such thing. However, there are some unexplained happenings at the old Quill and Scroll. Ghostly whispering, rattling grates, and other unexplained noises. At least, that's what she told me and Polly. I'm not sure what she's hearing exactly, but it's obvious she's worried." Harriet had no idea what was causing the commotion at the inn, but she knew it couldn't be blamed on ghosts. There had to be a logical explanation.

"Sounds like one of the typical things old buildings are noted for—the creaking, groaning, and cracking of old timbers. But I'll admit, it's hard to imagine what might be causing the whispering. That's too weird," her aunt said. "Perhaps it's nothing more than the wind whining through cracks around the windows and doors, or old timbers giving out a long squeak. It's quite an ancient building. I think it dates back to the eighteenth century."

Harriet nodded. "Polly told Celia the same thing about the noises, considering the age of the inn. We encouraged her to contact a building inspector to examine the fireplace and the walls again. Maybe even the roof and the cellar."

Aunt Jinny frowned. "Surely they did that before they purchased the place. It would have been foolish not to. One should at least inspect the foundation to make sure the inn doesn't come tumbling down around their ears."

"Celia said they did, but maybe something has happened to the building since then," Harriet suggested. "I was wondering if the Beems might have a bat problem. A large roost underneath the roof or in the chimney."

Her aunt laughed. "From ghosts to bats. You have quite an imagination, Harriet. It would take a lot of bats to make that kind of noise."

"That's just it," Harriet replied. "Sometimes a bat colony numbers in the hundreds, even thousands." She went on to explain what she'd learned on the internet and from Gavin about bats in the UK.

"And what sparked this sudden interest in bats?" Aunt Jinny asked.

"Will brought me one this afternoon. He found it in the church belfry," Harriet said. "I'm not sure what's wrong with it, or how much I'm allowed to do to help it. I've contacted the Bat Conservation Trust to see what to do about it. In the meantime, I'm keeping the little guy in the barn in an old birdcage."

"Well, do be careful handling it," her aunt said. "They can carry all kinds of communicable diseases. I don't want a case of human rabies on my hands."

"I promise I'm taking precautions," Harriet said. "Will is concerned about more bats in the church—understandably so. With all the legal protections in place for bats, a colony in the belfry may prove to be a long-term issue."

They reached town on their way to the Cliffside Chippy, their favorite fish and chips eatery by the shore. As they strolled past the Quill and Scroll, Harriet briefly toyed with the idea of dropping in to say hello to the Beems. But her stomach growled a protest, and she quickly decided against the idea. She did, however, admire the window boxes full of red and pink geraniums, which provided a nice splash of color against the dark stone of the inn's ancient, sea-battered walls. Besides, it was too nice an evening to be burdened with tales of woe—of jumping grates and moaning ghosts or even fluttering bats.

As she and Aunt Jinny ate their meal outside on the patio, Harriet could feel the tension in her neck and shoulders melting away. There was something about the sound of the surf and the smell of the sea that was as relaxing as it was invigorating. Children's laughter punctuated the cries of the gulls. How she loved summer in White Church Bay, where the breezes off the sea kept things from getting miserably hot but the sun still made its presence known.

Harriet noticed two men seated at a nearby table. They were so similar that they had to be twins. Brothers could look similar, but they were identical copies. Both were rather short, rotund, and completely bald. They even wore matching green jackets.

Small binoculars hung around their thick necks, possibly for birdwatching. Besides a wide variety of gulls, there were many shorebirds to admire—shearwaters, terns, gannets, and others. For those not interested in birds, there were porpoises, dolphins, whales, and seals to watch for too.

She wondered briefly if these men could be the Clutterbuck brothers Celia had mentioned earlier. Were they likely to play pranks on their hostess?

"It's not windy enough," Aunt Jinny said suddenly as she popped a fried potato wedge into her mouth.

"What?" Harriet asked.

Her aunt drew her attention to a young boy trying to fly a kite on the beach. He wasn't having much luck.

Harriet nodded as she took another bite of crispy fish doused with malt vinegar.

After their meal, Harriet and Aunt Jinny strolled along the beach for a while. Harriet pondered the tales she'd heard of pirates and smugglers. It boggled the mind to consider how many civilizations had settled in the area, from the ancient Romans to the Vikings to the Anglo-Saxons. The town was as rich in history as it was in natural beauty.

As the sun began to set, painting the sky with rich colors, their steps naturally turned toward home. Harriet smiled to herself as she realized her strides were less vigorous than those that had carried her into town. With her hunger sated and her mind relaxed, she was in less of a hurry.

Back at Cobble Hill Farm, Harriet hugged her aunt and returned to her own house. She stopped in the kitchen, wondering if she still had chamomile tea in the cabinet. Then she remembered the whimsical figurine Randy Danby had presented to her earlier in the day.

Glancing at the kitchen clock, she decided it wasn't too late to call her friend and neighbor Doreen Danby. In spite of her busy schedule with her farm, husband, and five children, Doreen had always made time to ensure that Harriet felt welcome in town, usually by inundating her with delicious baked goods.

Harriet retrieved her cell phone from her purse and tapped Doreen's name in her contact list.

"Good evening, neighbor," chirped Doreen's cheerful voice. "How lovely to hear from you."

"Hi, Doreen," Harriet replied. "How's your family? And the farm?"

"Tom is doing as well as he always does, but it helps that this year Thommy is stepping up with chores and responsibilities. Ava's been ever so helpful to me as well, and the younger ones seem to be staying out of trouble for once. Our animals are all doing well. We had a lamb who was limping for a bit, but Tom was able to treat that, and now we're right as rain. And the pets are all healthy, so really, I can't complain. How are you?"

"Busy, but well." Harriet came to the main point of her call. "Randy stopped by earlier today to bring me a present."

Doreen chuckled. "That boy is so sweet and thoughtful. He's always doing things like that."

"He learned it from his mother," Harriet said.

"What was the gift?" Doreen asked.

"I actually wanted to ask you about it. It's a porcelain figure of a dog. It looks old—maybe it's an antique. It seemed vaguely familiar to both Polly and me, but neither of us could figure out exactly where we've seen it before. I wonder if you have one like it."

"Did Randy say where he got it?" Doreen asked.

"I asked, but he just said he found it somewhere," Harriet said. "I'm a little concerned. If it's real Staffordshire porcelain, it could be quite valuable. Someone may have thrown it out, not realizing how rare it is." She didn't want to admit she had a sneaking worry that Randy might have plucked the little dog from his mother's display cabinet—or someone else's. Though she might be jumping to an unfair conclusion. He might have purchased the figurine after all, perhaps at a thrift shop.

"Yes, if it's Staffordshire, it could be expensive indeed," Doreen agreed in a musing tone. "Depending on when it was made and by who."

"That's what I thought," Harriet said. "It was a sweet gesture, but I can't accept something that might be worth a lot more than he got it for."

There was a long pause before Doreen hissed, "If that Gabriel Mellon has led Randy into stealing, I'm going to have Tom put them to work on the farm from sunup to sundown for the rest of the summer!"

CHAPTER SEVEN

Of all the things Harriet might have expected her friend to say, that hadn't been anywhere on the list. "That's a serious accusation, Doreen. I'm sure Randy wouldn't deliberately steal anything. You've raised your children well."

Doreen snorted. "Is there such a thing as *accidental* stealing?"

Harriet responded with a nonrhetorical question. "Who is Gabriel Mellon?"

"He's Donna Coomb's grandson, and a troublemaker through and through. His parents live in Liverpool, where Gabriel was expelled from school this past year. They sent him here for the summer so Donna can perhaps be a good influence on him." Doreen sighed heavily. "But from what I hear, Gabriel's not very trustworthy. Unfortunately, Randy has taken a keen liking to him, and they've spent much of their school holiday together. As an optimist, I hope that Randy is good for Gabriel, but now I'm concerned that Gabriel might be bad for Randy."

Harriet gazed at the hollyhocks through the kitchen window without really seeing them. The name Donna Coomb sounded familiar. Harriet thought she had something to do with numbers and accounts, maybe a local bookkeeper or bank teller. She worried that she'd stirred up a hornet's nest by calling Doreen about the figurine. What if Doreen accosted Donna without proof? It wasn't like her to fly off the handle, but her friend seemed truly upset. Maybe Harriet should have pressed Randy harder about where and how he'd obtained the little dog.

"Randy is a good boy," Harriet said. "I can't imagine him getting into the kind of trouble that Gabriel Mellon apparently has. Maybe your optimism will win out and Randy will have a positive impact on him. How old is Gabriel?"

"Thirteen, and much too streetwise as far as I'm concerned. I don't trust him. You know what they say about a bad apple ruining the others in the barrel. And to make matters worse, Ava thinks he's cute. The silly girl has lost her head over him. She's taken to riding her bike around with the two boys sometimes when she's not on a babysitting job or helping me at home."

"A summer crush, huh?" Harriet asked. It wasn't unusual for a thirteen-year-old girl to have one of those now and then. "This too shall pass."

"If so, the summer can't be over fast enough for me. I'm counting the days until Gabriel's parents take him back to Liverpool."

Unlike her friend, Harriet hoped the summer would pass at a leisurely pace. She loved summer and wanted it to linger. Besides, with only two months to go, she had too many wedding plans to finalize. She wanted to believe that Gabriel and Randy weren't up to anything more serious than boyish mischief. Of course, Harriet wasn't a parent, and Doreen was more likely to know what was going on with her son than Harriet was.

"Well, I don't think you need to worry about Randy," she insisted. "He's a good kid."

"I'm glad you think so, but I think I'll tell Tom to put our boy to work with more chores around the farm so he doesn't have so much time on his hands. I don't want Randy to get into trouble. And he will if he continues hanging around with Gabriel."

"Has Gabriel gotten into trouble since he came to the village?" Harriet asked. The new boy hadn't been arrested, or she would have heard that bit of news from Polly, if not Doreen. Surely Gabriel and Randy weren't doing anything illegal, were they?

"One of the constables caught him letting the air out of Poppy Schofield's tires. Just being ornery, I suppose. Van called Donna and told her to keep a closer eye on him. And Rand Cromwell caught Gabriel tossing pebbles at pigeons in the park and gave him a good tongue-lashing. You know Rand. He won't stand for abusing animals—not one bit."

Harriet did know. The local dogcatcher had a gruff exterior and a harsh manner, but he loved animals as much as Harriet did. She'd learned months ago that the man's bark was worse than his bite, and he'd recently adopted a dog in need.

"Sounds like boyish mischief to me," Harriet ventured, "not criminal activity."

Doreen sniffed. "That's where it starts. If left unchecked, I have no doubt it will become criminal. I don't want my Randy into that sort of mischief. There's a mean streak in Gabriel Mellon. How my sweet Randy and that boy have become best mates, I'll never understand. I'll find out where Randy got the figurine and get back to you."

"There's no rush. On the other hand, if he bought the little dog at a rummage sale and it's really an antique, I should perhaps return it to the original owner. I'm sorry if I worried you."

"I don't know a thing about antiques," Doreen admitted. "But you could check with Lloyd Throckmorton. He's the expert, as you know. Perhaps you might speak with Jane Birtwhistle too. She collects those little porcelain figures, as I recall."

Harriet made a mental note to speak with Jane and Lloyd. Lloyd owned an antique store and had a pet armadillo named Dottie. Harriet was surprised that she hadn't thought of him herself. He should be able to tell her if the dog figurine was the real thing or a knock-off.

"Don't worry about Randy," she told Doreen again. "I'm sure he didn't steal the dog. He wouldn't do that."

"He better not have," Doreen said. Harriet could hear a tremor of indignation in her friend's tone. "If there's anything I can't abide, it's a thief."

"Randy's a good boy," Harriet repeated. The more she thought about it, the more certain she was that Randy had discovered the item for sale somewhere. But why had he been reluctant to tell her exactly where he'd bought it? Had he gotten it somewhere his parents had forbidden him to go? Or perhaps he'd been out shopping or hanging with Gabriel when he should have been doing something else.

It was a puzzle for sure.

Friday morning, Polly arrived at the office with a white box. "I'll put the kettle on while you help yourself to one of the goodies in here," she told Harriet.

Harriet happily accepted. Anything from the Happy Cup Tearoom and Bakery was delicious. She picked out a small sponge cake with whipped cream in the middle. She closed her eyes after taking a large bite, relishing the sweetness. "Heavenly."

Soon the two of them were drinking tea and enjoying the baked goods. Between bites, they went over the schedule for the day. There was nothing out of the ordinary—the usual vaccines and a couple of routine examinations for two dogs, as well as a sick cockatiel. There was also a voice mail from a concerned farmer, who left his name and number, asking the vet to come see his donkey as soon as possible.

Harriet listened to the message twice and scribbled the information and directions to the farm on a pad of paper.

Polly licked cream off the tip of her finger. "What did Pastor Will bring you yesterday? I noticed the box lid had holes punched in it, so I'm guessing it was a small mammal, amphibian, bird, or reptile. Am I right?"

"Mammal," Harriet answered. "A bat. It's out in the barn."

Polly made a face. "I'm not fond of bats. What's wrong with it?"

Harriet shrugged. "I can't be sure. It's just a pup, I think. I've never treated a bat before. I checked on it first thing this morning, and it's still alive at least. I'm waiting to hear back from someone from the bat trust. Bats are a protected species, so there's a certain protocol to follow when treating them, and I don't know it. I don't want to make a mistake with an animal's health."

Raising an eyebrow, Polly said, "I vaguely remember your grandfather mentioning something about bats being protected by law. He never had a bat patient while I worked for him. So Will found it in the church belfry? I hope we don't find them hanging around the ladies' room or in one of the Sunday school classrooms. What a mess that would be!"

"Aunt Jinny said the same thing."

"If there's just the one, I suppose we don't need to worry too much," Polly ventured hopefully.

Harriet quirked an eyebrow. "Let's hope there's only one. Maybe it got lost from its colony somehow. I was wondering if the trouble at the Quill and Scroll could be caused by a bat colony. Do you think I should call Celia and suggest that?"

Polly shook her head. "Sure, there might be a few bats here and there in the old inn, but bats can't cause a grate to jump. I've been thinking about it too. I'm wondering if the noise has something to do with the increased lorry traffic on that street. You'd call a lorry a truck. And all the tour buses. Maybe the heavy traffic is jarring the building or the foundation or something."

Harriet agreed that was a possibility. She made up her mind to add that to her mental list of likely possibilities for the reason behind the noises at the inn. She'd been meaning to sit down and transfer that mental list to paper, but she hadn't gotten around to it yet.

Polly went on. "I was talking with Gran last night. She's staying with us for a while this summer. She thinks the Beems need to keep an eye on those twin twitchers—you call them bird watchers, right?"

"Why is she concerned about the Clutterbuck brothers? I think I saw them last night when Aunt Jinny and I went out for fish and chips. They hardly seemed threatening or dangerous in any way. I can't see them as pranksters."

"Gran thinks they're up to something other than watching shorebirds." She gave Harriet a knowing glance.

Harriet frowned. "Like what?"

"I don't know. Gran said she's seen them around town, taking photos here and there. Spies, maybe? Or private detectives. She said she saw them looking in someone's window with their binoculars."

"Spying on who? Or what? That's rather far-fetched." Harriet was puzzled by the idea. Most birdwatchers snapped photos and studied birds through their binoculars. If they were indeed private detectives, they weren't very inconspicuous. She'd never heard of detectives detecting in pairs. That would certainly draw unwanted attention.

Perhaps Polly's grandmother was merely the sort who didn't like strangers. Or maybe growing up in a town with a history of pirates and smugglers had predisposed her to be suspicious of others. Harriet wondered if perhaps she should have a word with Polly's grandmother to cover all the bases. She could ask her to describe exactly what she'd seen, and perhaps advise her to be careful about casting aspersions. After all, it was unfair of her to turn a town against two innocent tourists. On the other hand, if they weren't innocent…

"If your grandmother saw them doing something unlawful, she should call Van," Harriet said.

At the mention of Van's name, Polly's face lit up. "I haven't mentioned anything about Gran's suspicions to Van. He's been quite busy. With all the tourists and parking tickets and misplaced purses and temporarily lost children, he's had his hands full. Besides, Gran hasn't witnessed anything obviously illegal. She said they're nosy, that they write things down in their little notebooks, and aren't inclined to speak when passing on the sidewalk. They don't sound dangerous to me. I think they snubbed her, and she's offended."

"Maybe they're merely shy," Harriet suggested. "It seems to me that bird watchers, or twitchers, must make a lot of notes about the birds they see. I don't think your grandmother needs to be overly concerned."

"You're probably right," Polly admitted. "But who knows? They're staying at the inn, aren't they? Maybe they're the ones causing all the noise."

"But why? And how are they doing it without being caught?"

With a sigh, Polly replied, "I haven't a clue. But didn't Celia say she started hearing things around the same time the brothers registered as guests?"

"I think she did say something along those lines," Harriet conceded. "Could be a coincidence though."

"Sure, or maybe they're tapping on the walls and snooping around in the cellar for secret passageways or something."

Before Harriet could respond, her first patient of the day arrived—the cockatiel with a sinus infection. All thoughts of haunted inns and bat infestations were dismissed as she concentrated on helping the sick bird. It wasn't until much later in the day that her thoughts returned to the possibility that the Clutterbuck brothers might indeed be snooping around the inn, looking for something. But why? And what could they be looking for?

Driving back from the farm—where she'd diagnosed the sick donkey with a treatable respiratory infection, to the relief of the anxious owner—Harriet wondered if there might be a pirate stash or smuggled goods buried in the basement of the Quill and Scroll.

She was mulling this over when her cell buzzed on the seat beside her. It was Celia Beem. Harriet answered at once on the hands-free system. "Good morning, Celia."

"Harriet?" Celia asked rather breathlessly. "I know you're busy, but you did say you were a rather keen sleuth. I hate to impose on your time, but would you be able to come to dinner tonight at the inn? Freddie and I would be happy to host you and a guest—if you'd care to bring a friend or your fiancé. Our pork roast is rather exceptional, if I do say so myself."

"Has something happened?" Harriet asked. "Have you heard more strange noises?"

"We have," Celia replied, her voice tinged with panic. "And I'd value your insight."

"Did you call another building inspector?"

"Yes," Celia assured her. "He's coming first thing Monday morning."

"Shouldn't we wait to find out what he has to say?" Harriet asked. It was important to approach the situation in the most logical way possible.

"No, please do come tonight," Celia insisted. "Freddie wants to thank you in person for treating Scarlett. I know we talked about you coming tomorrow afternoon, but we'd like to see you tonight instead."

Harriet suppressed a sigh. It had been a long day. She'd meant to visit the inn, but she wasn't particularly interested in wandering around it today, listening to Celia's tales of ghostly laughter.

On the other hand, Harriet did enjoy a good pork roast. She felt certain Will would too. "Dinner sounds lovely. I'll be there."

Relief was evident in Celia's voice. "Oh, thank you, Harriet. Thank you so much. You're so kind." A time was set for dinner, and Celia promised the pork would melt in her mouth. "And there will be apple tart with custard sauce for pudding—I mean dessert. I think you Americans prefer that word, right? Dessert?"

"I'm getting used to it either way, and I'm rather fond of apple tart," Harriet assured her. "And afterward, remind me to speak to you and your husband about bat roosts. Some of the noises at your inn could possibly be caused by a large bat colony."

"Bats?" Celia's discomfort was evident in the single, barely whispered word.

CHAPTER EIGHT

White Church Bay
June 1941

"Dad, I'm going over to Miss Dingle's this afternoon. She's holding a special meeting of some sort. I'll take Jane with me." Flory finished washing up the lunch dishes and removed her apron. Then, unable to keep her questions to herself any longer, she asked, "Do you think the invasion is really going to happen? Will the Germans come to our village, or stay in London? How long do we have?"

"I reckon they'll take over the whole country sooner or later," her dad said glumly. "They took over the Channel Islands, didn't they?"

Flory felt a drop in her stomach. It was true. The Nazis now occupied Guernsey and Jersey. Who could have imagined it? The Germans had invaded the islands a year ago this very month, which meant they were less than twenty miles off the coast of the mainland. She supposed it was only a matter of time before they took over London—if a miracle didn't happen.

"Anyway, I reckon they'll try," her dad went on. "That's what they aim to do." His jaw tightened as he gazed toward the baby, sleeping peacefully.

Flory shuddered. It was too awful to even think about. "Do you think it will be soon? This summer maybe?"

Her father frowned. "Why these questions all of a sudden? Someone been talking at the Women's Institute about things they shouldn't?"

After clearing her throat, Flory replied, "The meeting at Miss Dingle's is about the invasion, about making preparations and such. We don't want to be caught off guard."

Dad stroked his stubbled chin. "What sort of preparations?"

"I couldn't say, because I don't know yet. But Miss Dingle seems to think we're in for it—and soon. Maybe by summer's end." Glancing at the clock on the wall, she added, "I need to get going. There are still a few chores to do, and I don't want to be late. Will you be at your meeting?"

He nodded as he rose from the table. "It's best that Miss Dingle leave worrying about that sort of thing to the Home Guard, and you can tell her I said so. We don't want her stirring up unnecessary fear. Don't need a lot of hysterical womenfolk fretting and crying over things that can't be helped."

Flory didn't know what to say. The Home Guard on the Channel Islands hadn't stopped the invasion there. She reckoned the Home Guard in White Church Bay wouldn't be able to stop the Nazis if they invaded their village either.

She thought of poor Donald out there on some foreign battlefield and said another prayer for his safety. She thought too of the vicar's sermon when he'd quoted St. Matthew, who encouraged Christians to pray without ceasing. Since becoming a mother during a war, Flory had learned the true meaning of those words.

After her father put on his cap and left, Flory made her way into the small parlor. Her back ached from leaning over the ironing board most of the morning. She looked forward to a few quiet moments of sitting. She scooped up Jane, who'd woken and begun to fuss, out of her pram. As she settled into the rocking chair, she kissed the top of Jane's downy head. How she loved this precious little girl. Her perfect baby.

Flory grimaced at the recurring thought of the Germans taking over her homeland. Tears came to her eyes, as they so often did these days. It was terrifying to consider how close the enemy really was. And what about those powerful warships and the submarines? U-boats, they called them. How many now lurked beneath the waves prowling the coastlines—perhaps right off the very shores of White Church Bay? The Home Guard regularly scanned the waters with binoculars for advance warning on incoming ships. But by the time a sub was spotted, would it be too late to stop an attack?

Flory forced the frightening thoughts from her mind. She snuggled the baby closer and thanked the Lord that they lived on the coast and not in London. She'd heard of whole families living in the underground stations in the city—their homes shattered with no hope of recovery. She also gave thanks for a happy, healthy baby and a house to share with her beloved father. They might not have everything they wanted, but they had everything they needed. It was pure selfishness to ask for much more.

After burping Jane and changing her, Flory took a few minutes to freshen up before leaving for the meeting at Miss Dingle's. As she ran a brush through her light brown hair, she regarded herself in the mirror. Who was that woman—not yet twenty-three years old—with dark circles under her eyes and worry lines around her mouth? She didn't want to look like an old hag when Donald returned home.

Flory pinched her cheeks to bring some color to her face.

After retrieving her well-worn hat from a peg by the door, along with her gas mask and Jane's smaller respirator, Flory carefully maneuvered the pram out the door and down the steps. She tucked a thin flannel blanket around the baby and then glanced at the sky, always fearing that one day she would hear the droning sound of a plane overhead. But it was blue and cloudless. Flory took a moment to give thanks for that too.

When Martin Quinn, the cobbler, ambled past her on the sidewalk, Flory acknowledged the elderly man with a nod. He'd retired some years ago, handing over his shop to his son to take over the shoe-repair business. But his son had been called up to serve, so the senior Quinn manned the shop once again. And business was booming. With new shoes and leather being rationed, Mr. Quinn's services were more in demand than ever. Flory was glad he was willing to do it, but it broke her heart to see a man who should be enjoying his well-earned rest put back to work.

Flory again pushed all unpleasant thoughts from her mind and focused on enjoying the walk, the fresh air, and stretching her legs. She watched the gulls reeling in the sky and admired the petunias in the Merritts' window boxes.

She received a warm welcome at Miss Dingle's charming little house. Leaving the pram outside the front door, she carried Jane inside, where she was quickly claimed by Mavis White for a cuddle. Several other women were present, most of whom Flory recognized. They all fussed over the baby.

Flory was aware of a dozen different conversations going on around her. Rationing seemed to be the most common topic. She tried to listen and learn. Frankly, she found the ration rules confusing and frustrating. She couldn't keep up with all the coupons and points. At first, they'd only had to be concerned about sugar, butter, and meat. Now rationing extended to cheese, bacon, eggs, and clothing. When would it all end?

Finally, Miss Dingle clapped her hands, calling the informal meeting to order. "Ladies, you may be wondering exactly why I've invited you here this afternoon."

Miss Dingle lifted her chin. "It is my belief we will be invaded sometime this year—surely while the weather holds. If my hunch is correct, we'll need to make certain preparations for our families, friends, and neighbors, as well as ourselves. We need to be ready."

"But what else can we do that we're not already doing?" one of the women asked, her tone laced with frustration.

Miss Dingle's lips pressed into a firm line, and she met the gaze of each woman in the room. "We need to begin hiding our most valuable possessions."

CHAPTER NINE

"Bats? In the chimney grate?" Freddie Beem frowned, his hands on his hips. The thirtysomething innkeeper had reddish-brown hair and a face dotted with caramel-colored freckles. Even his hands were freckled. The gap between his two front teeth gave him an endearing boyish appearance when he grinned.

However, he was not grinning now.

"It's a possibility," Harriet told him. "Will and I discussed the matter as we drove over here this evening. We think perhaps you should have the building inspector check for a roost when he comes on Monday. That could be what's causing all the commotion—bats coming and going."

She took a sip of water, patted her mouth, and placed her white linen napkin beside her plate. The meal had been delicious. She'd savored every bite. The pork roast was as succulent as Celia had promised, the vegetables well-seasoned and perfectly cooked. Harriet could tell by the way Will had been focused on his meal that he had enjoyed the food as well.

Harriet approved of the inn's dining room too. It was tastefully decorated with wood paneling, gleaming wood floors, and polished brass wall sconces. Fresh flowers in bud vases graced the tables, and a collection of large seashells brightened shelves around the room.

"I found a bat in the church's belfry this week," Will explained. "That's why we're suggesting you check for them on the premises. With all the caves around here, especially along the coastline, it shouldn't surprise us to find bats making their way into village businesses and even homes."

Freddie's frown deepened. "I can't imagine the noises Celia has described being caused by bats. They'd have to be as big as Scarlett." He chuckled.

"How is Scarlett?" Harriet asked.

Celia's expression lightened. "I think she's already feeling better. We have to keep her out of the kitchen and dining area, or else I'd ask if we need to bring her to you for another visit. She has the run of our private apartment, which has a doggy door to a fenced backyard. When our guests are agreeable, we often bring her into the parlor to entertain them. She's quite popular."

"I have no doubt," Harriet replied.

Will glanced at Harriet. "So your wife has heard the rattling grate, but you haven't?"

Freddie shook his head. "I have not."

"What about the voices?" Harriet pressed. "Celia thought she heard whispering and laughter. Have you heard anything like that?"

Freddie avoided his wife's penetrating stare. "Well, I heard *something*. It might have been voices. Then again, it could have been the wind blowing through the nooks and crannies. This place is drafty, you know. We've tried to plug up the chinks, but the inn is hundreds of years old. It's bound to creak and groan a bit."

"That doesn't explain the laughter." Celia crossed her arms as she stood beside their table, her face flushed, her mouth set in a stern line. Harriet could tell the young woman had grown tired of people doubting what she'd heard.

"And this is where you heard the noises?" Harriet asked, glancing around the dining room, which was filled to capacity with chatting diners. The bustling waitstaff were neatly attired in black slacks and crisp white shirts—none of the usual tavern maid costumes or pirate attire one often associated with historic seaside establishments like the Quill and Scroll.

"No, it was in the parlor. We use that room sometimes for private parties. The overnight guests often use it for reading and drinking a cup of tea before retiring for the evening," Celia explained. "I'll take you there as soon as you've finished your meal."

Will asked a few questions about the first building inspector's report. While he and Freddie discussed the subject, Celia excused herself to mingle with other customers. She exchanged a few words with a couple at the next table and gave quiet orders to one of the waitresses. This allowed Harriet time to watch other diners. She supposed some were locals while others were out-of-town visitors or tourists.

Again, she noticed the Clutterbuck twins. They sat in a far corner, eating in silence. No binoculars this time, but they wore identical sports jackets and khaki pants. An odd pair to be sure, but suspicious? The two men appeared to be quite harmless. What exactly did Polly's gran suspect them of?

Harriet made a mental note to learn more about the men. Perhaps she should introduce herself and ask if they were enjoying their visit. If indeed they were responsible for the strange noises that Celia heard in the parlor, what were they doing in there to cause such a ruckus? Had they found a hidden passageway or secret staircase? A tunnel leading to a smugglers' cave?

If the Clutterbuck brothers believed there was such a tunnel, why not inform the Beems and then ask permission to search for it? That would certainly be easier than sneaking around, hoping not to get caught in the act.

"I'm sorry to inconvenience you," Celia said, returning to their table, "but I can't stand not knowing exactly what's going on here at the inn. You understand, don't you? You will help?"

Harriet noted Celia's pale face, the persistent dark circles under her eyes. She sincerely hoped Aunt Jinny had recommended something soothing like chamomile tea to help her sleep. A hot bath by candlelight, accompanied by soothing instrumental music, was a good idea too. And Harriet's own mother always used a lavender-scented pillow for a good night's sleep.

"You aren't hearing the noises at night, are you?" Harriet asked, pushing her plate away.

Freddie glanced at his wife. "Celia said she heard the grate rattle one afternoon. The wind had kicked up, blowing in from the sea. I figured that was the cause of it." He gave Celia another sheepish look.

"I didn't say I heard any noises at night," she replied tartly. "It's in the daytime—mornings and afternoons—but there's no regularity to it. Freddie thinks I'm imagining things, but I'm not."

"Are the Clutterbuck brothers hanging around here at the inn during the day?" Harriet asked.

Celia shook her head. "They're out and about looking at birds. I suppose it's foolish to suspect them. They appear to be just what they claim: enthusiastic twitchers. So that brings us back to the possibility that someone is trying to scare us out of business."

"Who do you think would want to do such a thing?" Will asked gently.

Harriet had shared Celia's thoughts on the matter with him earlier, but it was obvious that Will wanted to hear what Celia had to say for himself.

"That Mackenzie woman," Celia replied promptly. She scanned the dining room as if to make sure she couldn't be overhead.

Harriet noted that the other diners continued with their meals. No one seemed to pay particular attention to the conversation at their table—not even the dubious Clutterbuck brothers.

"I don't believe I know a Mrs. Mackenzie. Or is it Miss Mackenzie?" Will glanced from Celia to Harriet.

"Mrs. Nettie Mackenzie. She owns the Pint Pot, that old inn on the road to Leeds. Not too many overnight guests, from what we've been told," Freddie said. "But she does a brisk lunch hour in the pub."

"I'm not familiar with her or her inn, but Polly said that your place is nicer," Harriet said. "Now that I've been here, I believe it. This is a top-notch establishment, and I'm sure other people feel the same way." It was hard to imagine a fellow business owner skulking around the Quill and Scroll, rattling grates and laughing maniacally to frighten the Beems out of business.

Celia nudged her husband in the ribs. "Go on. Tell them."

Freddie flexed the fingers of one hand. "Celia might have a point about Mrs. Mackenzie. She's hardly been welcoming, that's for sure. While we were still renovating, she came by a couple times and said some rather harsh things about us not being wanted here and that we should go back where we came from. That sort of thing."

"Now she's spreading nasty rumors about our kitchen being unsanitary and that our second-floor guest rooms are rat-infested." Celia folded her arms across her chest, eyes snapping with indignation.

"That's not kind or neighborly at all." Will took a sip of water and shook his head sympathetically.

"Perhaps you could keep track of where you hear the strange noises and at what time of day," Harriet suggested. "And make note of what you hear—grate rattling, voices, whispering, whatever."

Celia tipped her head. "Why?"

"Because then we can ask DC Worthington to look into Mrs. Mackenzie's whereabouts during those times. If she was someplace else with an alibi, then she's not likely to be the one trying to spook you," Harriet explained.

"She could be paying someone else to do it," Celia pointed out.

Harriet silently acknowledged this as a possibility. But why would the woman go to all that trouble?

Before she could mull it over too long, the waitress brought their dessert—the apple tart smothered with custard sauce. The Beems politely left Will and Harriet to enjoy the dish without being hovered over.

"Lovely old place," Will said, reaching a hand across the table to clasp one of Harriet's. "If the upstairs rooms meet with your approval, we could suggest that some of our out-of-town wedding guests stay here."

Harriet smiled. "If we get this cleared up. I don't want any laughing ghosts or jangling grates terrorizing our guests. And I don't want to see bats hanging from the rafters. If we don't solve the mystery here, it could prove bad for business. We've got to help the Beems, Will."

"Oh, I don't know," Will teased. "There are people who willingly pay for ghost tours and the like. Might be good for the Beems in the long run. Not that I believe in ghosts, mind you, nor would I encourage the Beems to lie about phantoms on the premises to drum up more business. But if word gets out, it might bring in more customers."

"They'll definitely need to quash any rumors about rats and unsanitary kitchen conditions," Harriet said. "Rumors like those can take on a life of their own and be very hard to disprove in the public eye."

"They can display certificates and that kind of thing," Will said.

"Right, but that only proves it to people who come through the door," Harriet reminded him.

"Well, love, you'd better solve the mystery and soon." Will gave Harriet a wink. Then he casually slipped the smiling young server a tip in appreciation of her cheerful service.

When they'd finished their dessert, Harriet caught Celia's eye and thanked her for a delicious meal.

"Would you like to see the parlor now?" Celia asked, her face alight with eagerness.

Harriet and Will agreed, so Celia led the way with Freddie bringing up the rear.

Harriet paused on the threshold to study the parlor. It was an attractive room with a gleaming wood floor and a floral area rug that complemented the wallpaper. It was smaller than the dining room but still large enough to entertain several guests.

The notorious fireplace was large and boasted a marble mantelpiece. Two leather sofas and several overstuffed chairs took pride of place. A huge potted fern loomed at one end of a storage bench with red velvet cushions next to the fireplace. Harriet wondered if they'd hired a professional for the interior decorating, or if Celia was simply this talented. Either way, it was a perfect hideaway for reading or enjoying a quiet conversation with other guests.

Will made his way to the fireplace. He pointed to the hearth. "So this is the noisy grate." He leaned over to peer up the chimney while Harriet perched on the bench.

"Yes, this is it," Celia answered with a reluctant laugh. "I haven't heard any noises today, thank goodness."

"Have any of your guests complained about hearing strange noises too?" Harriet asked.

"Heaven forbid!" Freddie said. "I hope not, anyway."

"No one has reported anything to me," Celia added.

"Would you mind if we examined your cellar?" Harriet asked.

Freddie arched an eyebrow. "There's nothing down there really—just storage."

"No tunnels or secret passageways," Celia assured them. "Freddie already checked."

"All the same, we'd like to poke around." Will gave them an encouraging smile.

"You take them, Freddie." Celia folded her hands together and sat next to Harriet on the storage bench. "I'll wait right here."

"Righto. This way then."

Harriet rose from her seat, wondering if Celia was afraid of something in the cellar. She herself wasn't fond of basements either. They were usually dark and dank. They tended to smell musty and have creepy shadows lurking in the corners. She was glad Will was with her as they made their way down the stairs. At one point, she thought she'd heard something and stopped to listen.

Will caught her elbow. "Not scared, are you, love?"

"No," Harriet said. "I thought I heard something, but I can't say what it was. And I'm not fond of cellars, generally speaking."

Freddie chuckled, obviously trying to put her at ease. "Nothing to fear down here, Doc. No pirate skeletons slumped along the walls or anything like that. We use it as storage for goods we buy in bulk. And the furnace, of course, plus a couple of chest freezers. That sort of thing."

When he flicked on the light switch, Harriet had to admit it was bright enough to see that there wasn't anything creepy at all. Nor did the cellar have an unpleasant smell. She saw nothing out of the ordinary—just several crates and boxes, shelves of canned goods, cider, and soft drinks.

"I know Celia is worried," Freddie said, "and I don't think she's imagining things. She's heard *something*. I'm sure of that. But as I said before, this place is over two hundred years old. Buildings like this shudder and creak all the time. Old timbers and whatnot."

Harriet nodded. The man didn't sound the least bit concerned. But how could they convince Celia there was nothing to be afraid of? "Are there earthquakes here?" she asked the two men.

Will's eyes widened. "Not that I recall."

"You think the grate rumbled because of earth tremors?" Freddie stood with hands on hips. "I've lived in the UK all my life and never heard of earthquakes along the coast. Nothing more disturbing than lorry traffic around here. What do you think? All the delivery trucks rumbling by—that could be causing the problem, right?"

"That's a possibility," Will agreed.

After exploring the cellar to satisfy their curiosity and finding no trace of hidden passages, Harriet and Will followed Freddie back upstairs to join Celia in the parlor once more.

"Find anything?" she asked anxiously.

"Not yet," Harriet told her. "I'm sure we simply haven't looked in the right place. When we do, the answer will be so obvious, we'll wonder how we missed it."

Her new friend bit her lip and nodded, but Harriet could tell Celia didn't quite believe her.

The Beems walked them to the front door of the inn.

"Thank you both for your excellent hospitality tonight, even though we weren't able to solve anything yet," Will said. "I'd like to return the favor by inviting you to services at White Church in town on Sunday. If you can get away, that is."

"And, Celia, I'd like to see the building inspector's report after his visit on Monday, if that's all right," Harriet added.

"I'll be sure to share that with you," Celia promised.

As Will drove Harriet home, he said, "I think Celia was disappointed we didn't find anything that would explain the noises. She was probably hoping we'd hear something for ourselves."

"Yes, I got the same impression," Harriet agreed. "But Freddie is right. Old places groan and creak. When the wind blows down the chimney or around the window casements, perhaps it makes a vague whispery sound like muttering voices."

"On the other hand, if Nettie Mackenzie, or someone acting in her stead, is making mischief for that young couple, she must be stopped," Will added.

Harriet nodded. She'd already made up her mind to get to the bottom of it, whatever *it* was.

CHAPTER TEN

During a break in her appointments Saturday morning, Harriet hurried over to Thistle and Thatch, the antique shop owned by Lloyd Throckmorton. When she showed the whimsical dog figurine to Lloyd, he peered at it through his rimless glasses and stroked his short gray beard.

"Is it worth anything?" she asked.

"Indeed it is." Lloyd ran a thin finger along the length of the porcelain figurine. "See, it's been salt-glazed, which was done in the early 1700s, and the gilding shows evidence of aging. They would fire the pottery at a high temperature and cover it with salt while it was still hot to form a protective coating. Where did you get this?" He regarded her thoughtfully.

Harriet hesitated briefly before saying, "It was a gift."

"It's quite a gift. Staffordshire figurines like this one have been prized for years by many faithful collectors. Modern forgeries abound, however, so you can't be too careful. Animals are very popular, especially dogs. I sold one a couple of months ago—a greyhound."

"Can you tell me what it sold for?" Harriet asked, all but holding her breath.

He met her gaze. "A little over three hundred pounds."

Even though Harriet thought she'd sufficiently braced herself, it took her a few seconds to recover her powers of speech. "I see," she said. "Do you have any like this one in the store?" She glanced around at merchandise on display.

"Nothing this old. Why? Are you interested?" A hopeful gleam lit his face.

Harriet smiled. "No. I was hoping to find something to compare this one to, to figure out whether it's the real thing or a knock-off."

"I can answer that for you. It's the real thing," Lloyd assured her. "If you decide to start collecting these, come see me. Or talk with Jane Birtwhistle. She has a fine collection."

"I might do that," Harriet replied. She thanked him for his time and then carefully rewrapped the figurine, slipping it into the tote bag she carried with her.

As she hurried along the sidewalk back to where she'd parked her vehicle, she noticed Van Worthington near the World War I monument talking with two tourists. Well, she assumed they were tourists. They had impressive cameras hanging around their necks, and one of the men clutched a map in his hands. Van pointed toward something near the shore, apparently giving directions as well as answering questions. Harriet waited until the pair thanked him and hurried away before she approached the detective constable.

"Good morning, Van. Another busy day for you, I see." Harriet smiled at him warmly.

Van touched the brim of his hat. "Hello, Harriet. Every day is a busy day."

"Got a minute?" she asked.

"Always for you," he replied with a grin. He peered at her face. "You've been sleuthing again, haven't you? We're going to have to make you an honorary member of the force."

"No thank you," Harriet replied. "I'll keep it to a hobby. You can tell I'm sleuthing just by looking at me?"

Van laughed. "I was winding you up. Polly mentioned something about you having caught a scent recently. Anything you need official support with?"

"Not yet. I haven't discovered enough to figure out if there's any criminal activity. But if I find some, I'll loop you in. I'd appreciate being able to bounce some ideas off you though."

He gestured for her to go ahead.

She launched into a summary of Celia Beem's claims about the strange noises at the inn. "Any idea what might be causing those?"

Van frowned. "Why hasn't she called the station if she's concerned about possible intruders? We'd be happy to look into the matter."

Harriet shrugged. "I think she's embarrassed. She suggested the old inn might be haunted, though she doesn't actually believe that."

Van's eyebrows shot up. "Ghosts are out of my jurisdiction for sure. Never heard tell of the place being haunted. Old timbers make noise all the time. Could that be what's causing it?"

"That seems to be the most popular theory so far," Harriet said. "But could there be any possibility that someone might be trying to scare them into leaving town?"

"Who would want to do that?" Van asked.

"Maybe someone who feels her livelihood is threatened by their doing well at the new inn," Harriet suggested. "Someone like Nettie Mackenzie?"

Van mulled that over then seemed to dismiss the idea. "Nettie's not the cheeriest soul in town, but she'd hardly creep around trying to scare someone into closing a business. We've never had any legal trouble with her. She's a widow, and tough enough to know how to keep her customers in line." He placed his fists on his hips. "What nonsense! Who came up with that idea?"

Harriet shrugged. "The Beems insist she's been quite rude to them."

"She's rude to everyone. And when she's not rude, she's grumpy. Frankly, I'm surprised she's stayed in business this long. But her prices keep some people coming back."

"I'm just trying to help Celia and Freddie figure out what's going on." Harriet shifted her tote bag from one shoulder to the other.

Van pursed his lips then said, "I might have an idea about the noise. Sergeant Oduba and I made an arrest the other night at a row house behind the inn, one street over. A couple of thugs have been stealing car parts from rental vehicles—hubcaps, catalytic converters, that sort of thing. Easy to transport and to sell. Maybe they've been trespassing on the old inn property too. I should take a look. When we took those goons into custody, we didn't confiscate as many items as we expected to find. Maybe they've stashed the loot somewhere on the Beems' property."

Harriet felt her mood lift. Van's idea had merit. It was certainly more logical than ghosts. "I'm sure they'd appreciate your attention on the situation. Celia is beside herself. Tell them about the arrest. It would put her mind at ease if you did find stolen goods on their property. I hadn't thought about trespassers of that kind."

"Yes, ma'am." Van's eyes danced with good humor. "I'll drop in on them today after I get a bite to eat and pick up the sergeant."

Harriet returned home, still curious about the dog figurine but somewhat relieved about the Beems' situation. She promptly took Maxwell for a romp in the garden. After checking on the bat in the barn and refilling the tiny water dish inside the birdcage, Harriet felt a strong urge to meet Nettie Mackenzie. Even though Van had assured her the woman was a law-abiding citizen, Harriet wanted to form her own opinion of the grouchy innkeeper.

It was nearly one o'clock when she called Will and invited him to lunch at the Pint Pot.

"I'm not sure I can," he hedged. "It's not that I don't want to, but I haven't quite finished my sermon for tomorrow. I'm suffering a bit of preacher's block, I'm afraid."

"Even a pastor has to eat," Harriet reminded him. "Besides, stepping away for a break might get the gears turning again."

"When you put it that way, it sounds like I'd be shirking my duty if I refused," he said with a chuckle. "All right. Let's do it."

The Pint Pot lacked the homey charm on display at the Quill and Scroll. Dark and gloomy, it smelled of stale beer, old smoke, and overcooked cabbage. Harriet wrinkled her nose as she and Will paused inside the door to allow their vision to adjust from the summer sunshine to the dimness within. No polished waitstaff greeted them as they entered.

A middle-aged woman with brown hair streaked with gray stood like a sentinel behind the long bar. Harriet guessed she must be Nettie. The only other female in the place was a teenage girl wearing faded jeans and an oversize blue T-shirt. Harriet quickly realized she'd been right—the only thing she liked about the Pint Pot was the lovely purple clematis climbing up the brick wall outside.

Will escorted her to a table near a small grease-streaked window, and she was grateful for his grounding presence at her side. Every head turned, watching the newcomers with open curiosity. Mostly truck drivers, Harriet guessed, based on the number of vehicles parked outside. Harriet and Will exchanged a poignant glance.

When they sat down, Harriet leaned toward Will and whispered, "Maybe it wasn't such a good idea to come here after all." She cringed at the sticky oilcloth in an unappealing shade of green that served as a table covering. "I've already lost my appetite."

The woman stepped out from behind the bar and headed for their table, her pinched expression neither curious nor welcoming.

Harriet was suddenly overwhelmed by the desire to demand to know whether Nettie was the one terrorizing Celia. She couldn't shake the words from her mind, though she knew it would be unwise, even counterproductive, to use such a direct approach.

As if he sensed her internal struggle, Will saved her. He gave Nettie his kindest smile, one Harriet had seen melt the coldest features. "Good afternoon."

Nettie didn't even crack a smile in the face of Will's charm. "What brings you in today?" she demanded. Her gaze flickered to Will's pastoral collar.

Obviously, Celia and Freddie hadn't been exaggerating when they spoke about Nettie's rude manner. But, Harriet reminded herself, that didn't mean she was responsible for the odd noises at the inn.

"We heard you serve a nice lunch," Will said. "What's today's special?"

The woman regarded them skeptically. "No special. Just the usual ploughman's lunch." She was referring to a meal, usually cold, that included bread, cheese, and onions.

"That's fine," Will told her. "I'll also have a pot of tea. Harriet, what would you like?"

"Orange squash, if you have it," Harriet said, craving something sweet after Nettie's sour welcome. She'd come to enjoy the beverage, usually made with fruit juice, water, and some kind of sweetener. "Are you Nettie Mackenzie?"

"That's Mrs. Mackenzie to you," the woman snapped. She eyed Harriet with a critical eye. "You must be the lady veterinarian who took over Old Doc Bailey's practice. I've heard about you."

Harriet couldn't help wondering what she'd heard. Forcing herself to respond cheerfully, she replied, "Yes, I'm Harriet Bailey. Dr. Bailey was my grandfather."

"You're a Yank." It was a statement, not a question.

"Guilty as charged," Harriet said. "I was born and raised in Connecticut." She gestured around the dining room. "Is this your establishment?"

Nettie narrowed her eyes. "It is." Her tone was challenging, as if she wanted to add, *What's it to you?*

"I'm Pastor Will Knight," Will chimed in. "I don't believe we've met."

"We haven't." With that the woman spun on her heel and made her way to the kitchen.

"Not the warmest person I've ever met," Harriet murmured.

"That's an understatement," Will replied with a small smile.

Before they could carry on their conversation, the teenage girl arrived with a tray. She eyed them with interest as she placed a bottle of orange squash and an empty glass in front of Harriet.

"Good afternoon. What's your name?" Will asked as the girl put a small brown teapot along with a cup and saucer in front of him.

"Phoebe." The girl had large brown eyes, heavily fringed with thick, dark lashes.

"Are you Mrs. Mackenzie's daughter?" Harriet asked.

"She's my aunt," Phoebe replied.

"Working through the summer?" Harriet couldn't guess how old the girl was—anywhere from sixteen to her early twenties.

"I work here all year round," Phoebe told her. "And have done since I was sixteen."

Harriet saw an opening. "Then you must be able to manage the place single-handedly when your aunt is away."

Phoebe frowned. "Aunt Nettie is never away. She's here night and day. Lives upstairs. Can I get you anything else?"

"No thank you," Will assured her. "Our lunch is on the way." As Phoebe retreated with her tray in hand, he chuckled. "Subtle, Harriet."

Harriet feigned an offended sniff. "What? It's not like I asked Nettie herself. Or rather, Mrs. Mackenzie. And now we know the woman is a slave to her business. She probably didn't creep undetected into the Beems' parlor to rattle the grate. But she may have paid one of her regular customers to do it for her."

Will regarded the other customers. "I doubt it. None of them seem desperate."

"You don't have to be desperate to appreciate a little extra jingle in your pocket," Harriet pointed out.

Nettie returned with two large oval plates, set one in front of each of them without a word, and stalked away again.

Harriet took in the two thick slices of whole wheat bread, ham and cheese slices, miniature pots of mustard and chutney, some pickled onions, and a hard-boiled egg. It wasn't as impressive as Celia's food, but it seemed hearty.

Will reached for Harriet's hand, bowed his head, and said a quiet blessing over the food. When she raised her head, Harriet noticed others in the room staring at them openly as though they'd sprouted two heads on their shoulders. She supposed there weren't too many Pint Pot customers who said grace before they ate.

She also noticed Mrs. Mackenzie drilling them with a sharp glare. Harriet forced herself to smile, although she felt it was a feeble attempt at best. Phoebe said her aunt worked all the time. It wasn't likely that Nettie would sneak away during the afternoon, creep into the parlor at the Quill and Scroll and make groaning noises to scare Celia Beem out of business. Van had been right.

Harriet turned her attention to her food, which she ate without much enthusiasm. The bread was stale. The ham had been sliced so thin she thought she'd be able to see through it if she dared lift it from the plate to hold it to the light. She apologized to Will for making him come.

"I'm just glad you didn't come alone," he said softly. Then, noticing that she had only picked at her food, he added, "The mustard and chutney help. We don't want to offend our hostess." He made a sandwich of the items on his plate and took a bite.

Harriet followed suit. "Considering the lovely meal we enjoyed last night at the Quill and Scroll, I don't think the Beems need to worry about this place providing any competition. I do understand why Nettie hasn't been thrilled about their arrival."

"I do too."

As they ate, Harriet was ever mindful of Nettie's scalding glances from behind the bar as she waited on other customers. "I think Mrs. Mackenzie is suspicious of our intentions," she murmured to Will.

"It seems like it," he agreed. "Although what she suspects us of is anybody's guess."

As they ate their meal, Harriet shared with him what Van had told her earlier about the grumpy innkeeper. "He said she might be the rudest woman in town, but she's a law-abiding citizen all the same. Van seemed astonished that anyone would think she might be responsible for trying to spook the Beems out of business."

"Then I suppose she's guilty of nothing more than rudeness and poor cuisine. Neither are illegal."

"I think perhaps she's a workaholic if she never leaves the inn, as Phoebe said."

"Perhaps she doesn't trust anyone else to run the place," Will ventured.

"So it's not likely that she's our culprit."

Harriet saw Nettie presenting a tab to a man in the far corner. The innkeeper slouched as she spoke with him. Neither smiled. Harriet wondered if he was a regular or someone who'd ventured in for the first time. If so, she doubted he'd ever come back. She didn't intend to.

"Still, I suppose she could have paid someone to pull the pranks for her," Will proposed. "Someone other than her customers."

"We may be barking up the wrong tree entirely." Harriet drained the last bit of her orange squash. "Van mentioned an arrest he and Sargeant Oduba made in one of the row houses behind the inn. He said some men had stolen car parts and were hiding them there. Maybe they're the ones making the noises Celia hears. Van said they might have even trespassed on the Beems' property. He's going to look around to see if they might have stashed anything there."

Will sat back in his chair, pushing his plate away. "That might be the explanation."

Before Harriet could respond, Phoebe came over to place their bill on the table and whisk their plates away.

With a twinkle in his eye, Will said, "I think they want us to be gone." He reached for his wallet. "I need to get back to the rectory anyway. Have to finish my sermon. You were right about the break being what I needed." He placed some cash on the little tray.

Harriet considered protesting. She'd invited him, so she should pay. But she also knew him well enough to know that he wouldn't hear of it. So instead she said, "Thanks for coming with me, Will. You're a good sport."

He squeezed her hand. "I'll be your sleuthing sidekick anytime."

Even as Harriet returned his smile, she had to wonder how good her sleuthing skills really were. After all, she'd already been on the case for days, and she felt as if she was no closer to solving it than when she'd started.

CHAPTER ELEVEN

White Church Bay
June 1941

Her father was in a bit of a sulk when Flory arrived home late that afternoon. He'd put the kettle on, made himself some tea, and put away her ironing board. He muttered gruffly about wanting something to eat.

Flory quickly removed her hat and went about rustling up a meal. She refilled the kettle, silently thanking the Good Lord that Jane was fast asleep in her pram. The meeting at Miss Dingle's home had gone on much longer than Flory had expected. But there had been so much to talk about, so many questions that needed to be addressed.

It had been a serious meeting, one that called for quiet reflection. Flory remembered when everyone used to say, "If the Germans come." Now everyone said, "When the Germans come." It was such a small change, that single word, but it unnerved her.

"Been working myself to the bone most of the day," Dad muttered. He drained the last of his tea, and Flory hastened to refill his cup. "Can't imagine what you ladies had to talk about that took so long."

Her conscience pricked, Flory turned up the heat on the large pot at the back of the stove to bring the thick soup to a boil again. It was heaped with chunks of potatoes and vegetables from their own garden. She'd seasoned the soup with a piece of bacon rind and thought it tasted fine. "What have you been doing, Dad?" she asked.

"Fixing the west end of that stone wall behind the church," he replied. "Vicar's been worried it might fall. Could hurt somebody if they got too near." He sniffed. "You weren't in when I got home, so I took the hoe to that last row of cabbages. I've got Home Guard tonight. Need to report in an hour or so."

"Sorry, Dad." Flory remained silent as she set the kitchen table. No matter what she told him about the discussion at Miss Dingle's, he'd take exception to it.

"Why were you meeting about an invasion anyhow?" He scowled at her beneath his shaggy eyebrows. "What's Edith Dingle stirring up now? Served tea and crumpets, did she? Had a regular tea party there, all you ladies?"

Flory replied with a straight face. "We had ersatz coffee and carrot fudge."

Her father looked aghast. "Carrot fudge? Now that's carrying it a bit too far."

When Flory laughed to make it obvious she was joking, Dad's mouth quirked up into a crooked grin. The tension between them dissolved, and she smiled, breathing a sigh of relief. She preferred their home to be peaceful, especially with life hanging in the balance all over the world. It felt as if their house was a safe haven from all of that. "We had tea and bread with jam. Nothing fancy."

"What did you talk about?"

"The possibility of invasion and the horror stories coming from Poland about what the Nazis have done there," Flory said. Then she bit her lip and decided to come clean. "Miss Dingle suggested we start crating up our valuables to hide."

Her dad snorted. "What valuables?"

"Mum's Staffordshire figurines, for one. They're valuable antiques. She told me so." The collection of porcelain figurines had been in her mother's family for years.

Dad pressed his lips together but didn't argue.

Flory went on. "Some of the women think we should also hide items that are in short supply, like torch batteries, hairpins, elastic for sewing, and such. Maybe even a saucepan, if we have one to spare. Who knows when those things will be manufactured again? Plus, coin collections and jewelry, of course." Flory ladled out a bowl and carried it to her father.

"And where does she suggest we hide these valuables?" her father grumbled, accepting the bowl of soup she offered him.

"In the old smugglers' tunnels." Flory cut a slice of the hearty bread she'd made before she left and handed it to him as she shared everything that Miss Dingle had told them about the proposed hiding places.

Her father said, "My grandfather used to tell me how the boats came in at low tide and men unloaded goods into caves and cellars. Some of the oldest homes in town have secret passageways that connect one house to another. The old pub too, down near the shore. That way the contraband could be moved from place to place if the officials got suspicious."

"Miss Dingle suggested the Home Guard may want to use some of the old passageways to hide supplies in—just in case. She says no one wants to be caught napping if the Nazis land on the shore." Flory rambled on, mindful of her father's silence.

Would he consider it all an unnecessary precaution, even a foolish one? Flory wanted to protect her mother's beloved little figurines, especially the dogs. Those had been Mum's favorite. They'd belonged to her own mother and her grandmother before that. Mum had been so fond of those whimsical figurines.

Yes, Flory would wrap each one carefully to hide away. Maybe she'd keep one of the King Charles spaniels on the mantelpiece. Flory didn't know exactly how much they might be worth. She'd never thought to ask. But whatever their monetary value, she could never replace their sentimental value. She couldn't risk anything happening to them.

After he'd taken the edge off his hunger, her father asked, "I suppose the ladies are going to crawl into those tunnels with their bits and bobs to hide them? Slippery dark places, I imagine. And who knows if the old walls are stable?" he added. "I don't want you to go down there, Flory. If anything needs hiding, I'll do it myself."

"All right, Dad." Flory didn't want to stoke his ill humor again.

As Flory sat at the table with her own bowl of soup and slice of bread, she asked, "Dad, is there anything you might want to protect from the Germans? What about your watch?" She indicated the pocket where he kept his timepiece. It had been a gift from his father when he'd turned twenty-one. Flory had never known him to be without it.

"I'll have to think on it," he mumbled with his mouth full. He quirked his head to one side. "It's beginning to rain." He sighed. "I'll need to get my oilskins and gum boots before I go on duty." He finished his meal and pushed his bowl away. Rising from the table, he ordered, "You stay in tonight."

"I will," Flory promised. She glanced out the kitchen window. The sky was clouding up, and a drizzle of rain dotted the window.

"And don't forget to pull the blackout curtains." His tone was stern. "Don't want to pay a fine."

"I won't forget." Flory's gaze flickered to the heavy black sateen curtains she'd had to sew for each window in the house. Ugly, but mandatory for blackout conditions. Two shillings a yard. Some families hadn't been able to purchase the cloth and had opted for black paper instead.

Still grumbling, her father finished wrapping himself for the weather and stumped out the door into the rainy night.

Jane began to fuss. Flory hurried to pick up the baby and then cradled her in the crook of her arm, murmuring soothingly to her. She touched her daughter's downy head with the tips of her fingers. The child was finally getting a bit more hair, and it looked as if it might be white-blond. Flory hoped it would be curly, not straight as straw like her own. Either way, her daughter was beautiful. When she held out a finger, the baby clasped it. Such a precious child.

Flory carried Jane to her bedroom to change her nappy. Then she sat down in the old maple rocking chair to nurse her. Rain pelted the windows in earnest now. Poor Dad, working outside. Poor Donald, wherever he was.

The tears started, as they had so many times before. She was heartily sick of the war, the rationing, the constant knitting and mending. And now clothes rationing too. That had been a heated topic of discussion that had made the meeting go on longer than anticipated. Flory knew she mustn't complain when so many lives were worse than she could even imagine. But before this, a new dress had been one of her favorite ways to cheer herself. How she missed the small comforts she had never fully appreciated before.

A loud knock at the door snapped Flory out of her thoughts. Who could be venturing out in the rain at the supper hour? She hadn't turned on the lights yet, so surely it wasn't a warden come to chastise her. She placed the baby safely in the crib, removed her apron, and went to open the door.

Marietta stood on the doorstep, huddled in a rain slicker, a scarf covering her head.

Flory opened the door wide and ushered her friend into the house, leading her to the kitchen. "What on earth are you doing out there in the rain at night?" she demanded. "You could have slipped off the curb and broken an arm or leg."

Chuckling, Marietta divested herself of her coat and scarf. She handed them to Flory, who hung them on a peg near the kitchen door. "It's not quite that dark yet. What smells so good?"

"Soup," Flory replied. "Want some?"

"I won't say no," her friend replied. No one turned down the offer of a meal these days, no matter how humble the food.

Flory urged Marietta to have a seat. She dished up a bowl of the savory soup and placed it before her. Then she hurried to clear the dishes for the meal she'd shared earlier with her father.

"This is delicious," Marietta declared. "You've done so much with so little."

Flory flushed with pride. There was nothing she liked better than praise for her cooking, unless it was people admiring her little daughter. She pushed the bread plate toward Marietta along with the jar of strawberry preserves. Her father hadn't eaten the apple cake, so she offered that to her friend as well.

"Tea?" she asked, reaching for the kettle.

Marietta shook her head. "No, this is more than enough. I didn't intend to come over and eat you out of house and home. Did your father go on duty tonight?"

"He did, so you may speak freely," Flory told her. "I assume you came to talk about something urgent or private. Maybe something that was brought up at the meeting?"

With a shrug, Marietta said, "Perhaps. It's about hiding our valuables in the smugglers' tunnel. I've been thinking long and hard about that since leaving Miss Dingle's."

Flory sat down at the table. She raised an eyebrow. "And?"

"I don't think we should put all our eggs in one basket, if you know what I mean." Marietta gave her a searching look. "I have another idea."

CHAPTER TWELVE

After doing a load of laundry and answering emails from her parents and her friend Ashley in the States, Harriet fixed herself a large snack of cheese and crackers, an apple, and a cup of rice pudding. The lunch at the Pint Pot had hardly been filling or satisfying, so she was still hungry. Poor Will was probably suffering from hunger pangs too. She should have invited him to stay at her house for an apology lunch.

Harriet felt a tug of disappointment that there'd been no response from the Bat Conservation Trust regarding what to do about the little bat in the barn. She knew she'd hear from them as soon as they were able. In the meantime, she'd been relieved to read on the trust's website that there was little risk of rabies transmission but that she'd been right to wear gloves and a mask while examining the bat. Because it had so little fur, Harriet felt certain it was a baby. And, also according to their website, she was doing the right thing by keeping it in a safe, quiet, and dark place until someone from the trust came to claim it. She was anxious to have it in the correct hands.

As she nibbled, slipping a bit of cheese to Maxwell, who hovered at her ankle, she considered what Lloyd had told her about the charming little porcelain dog. She wondered if Doreen had found a chance to talk to Randy about where he'd obtained the figurine. Summer was the usual time for tag sales, church bazaars, and rummage sales, so it was possible he'd bought the dog for mere pennies. Harriet had heard more than once about people selling objects d'art for far less than what the items were worth simply because they didn't know the actual value. Harriet couldn't believe that Randy might be a thief.

Would Jane Birtwhistle know of a likely place where Randy might have come by the figurine? Perhaps, as a collector, she kept her finger on the pulse of the market. It seemed likely, since the retired teacher was well-organized and usually up on the news.

Opening her refrigerator to retrieve a carton of milk, Harriet took note of several essentials that she was nearly out of. Perhaps it would be a good idea to run to the store and visit Jane at the same time.

She made up her mind to drive back into town. After a quick phone call to Jane to make sure she was up for an impromptu visit, Harriet was on her way with both a grocery list and the little dog figurine tucked into her large purse. She rolled down the window on the Land Rover's driver's side, relishing the warm summer breeze on her face.

Harriet had barely rounded the first bend when she noticed two boys on bicycles pedaling her way. She recognized the shorter of the two as Randy Danby. Sounding her horn with one hand, she waved out the window with the other.

Randy raised a hand to wave back. She guessed the taller boy with tousled blond hair was the notorious Gabriel Mellon. He gave her a bold stare when she stopped her vehicle in the middle of the road. The boys appeared to be headed to the Danby farm. Perhaps Doreen was putting them to work with Tom.

"What are you boys up to this afternoon?" she asked through the open window. "Helping out on the farm?"

Randy nodded. Then he gestured to his friend. "This is Gabriel. He's here for the summer. Gabriel, this is Dr. Bailey, the one I told you about."

"Hi, Gabriel. I've heard about you." Harriet flashed him a smile.

The boy's eyes widened before a slight frown wrinkled his brow. "Hiya," was all he said.

"You two will have to come over some time to see the baby bat I'm taking care of," she said. "But call first."

"Sure, okay," Randy said, an eager expression on his freckled face. "I've never seen a bat up close before. Have you, Gabe?"

Gabriel shook his head. "Got any other animals at your place?"

Harriet smiled. So, the boy liked animals, did he? "I have a cat named Charlie and a dog named Maxwell. He's a dachshund whose hind legs were paralyzed when he was hit by a car. But he still gets around with a wheeled prosthesis."

Randy laughed. "Yeah, it always reminds me of training wheels on a bike. And sometimes she has animals boarding at her place like donkeys, llamas, and alpacas."

Harriet was quick to note the look of interest on Gabriel's face. Perhaps he wasn't so tough after all. "Well, I must be going. See you later. Remember, call before you come." Harriet waved and drove on.

She watched through her rearview mirror as the boys pedaled toward the farm. Gabriel hardly seemed like a major criminal. More like a bored kid with a mischievous streak. And an interest in animals. She had a hunch Tom and Doreen could keep him in line.

She toyed with the idea of taking Gabriel to meet Clarence Decker. The teen had a knack with animals and was always bringing home strays, caring for injured rabbits, dogs, cats, and any other creature that came his way. It might be a good thing if Clarence, who was older and more mature, took both Randy and Gabriel under his wing for part of the summer. He could put them to work cleaning cages and learning how to treat sick animals. Something to consider.

Minutes later, she knocked on Jane Birtwhistle's front door. The elderly woman greeted her with a warm and eager smile. She wore a floral seersucker dress, and her gray hair was neatly arranged. Several cats of assorted colors peered through the door too, curious about the newcomer. Harriet immediately recognized Mittens, Jane's black-and-white tuxedo cat. The others were familiar too, all former strays. Jane attracted them like a magnet and cared for them beautifully.

"Come in, Harriet," Jane urged. "I put the kettle on as soon as you called. It's so nice to have company. I also have a fresh honey-spice tea loaf. You must try it. It's an heirloom recipe."

Following Jane's lead, Harriet stepped gingerly, trying not to smash a paw or a tail, even as meowing cats twined around her ankles. "Sounds delicious," she replied, making her way carefully to the sofa in the sitting room.

It was a modest home with several bookcases crammed with books of all shapes, sizes, and subjects—appropriate for a retired schoolteacher. Jane had been born and raised in that house. With one glance around the room, Harriet realized it was filled with memories. It smelled of cinnamon without a hint of the unpleasant odors that often accompanied a multicat home.

"That's enough, my dears. Give poor Harriet space to breathe." Jane clapped her hands, which sent the cats scattering. "I'll bring in the tea."

Mittens came over and rubbed against Harriet's hand, purring loudly. She'd once treated him for hyperthyroidism, a disorder of the thyroid gland. He refused to take pills, so Harriet had used an ear paste instead. His social obligations fulfilled, Mittens jumped over the back of the sofa and disappeared.

Harriet smiled. Cats had minds of their own. She set the boxed figurine on the coffee table. Her eyes were drawn to two similar figures on the mantel over the fireplace—a dog and a horse. The whimsical dog was almost identical to the one she'd brought with her.

Jane returned with the tea tray. The perfect hostess, she served the tea with milk and sugar and offered Harriet a slice of what appeared to be pound cake. The sweetness of the cake was balanced by earthy spices, and it was dense and moist.

"What did you call this?" she asked between bites. "It's delicious."

"Honey-spice loaf. My mother's recipe." Jane flushed with pleasure at the compliment.

They exchanged pleasantries about the summer weather and various church activities. After a few minutes Jane asked, "You said you had something to show me, Harriet. Is that it?" She indicated the box with a slight frown. The words *Hypodermic Needles* were clearly printed on the side.

"I didn't bring needles, of course," Harriet hastened to assure her. She placed her empty plate on the table and reached for the box. After opening it, she carefully withdrew the figurine, which she handed to Jane. "I see you collect similar pieces." She thrust her chin toward the mantel where a few figurines were displayed.

Jane admired the little dog. "I do. This is a King Charles spaniel. Do you collect them too?"

"No, it was given to me as a gift," Harriet replied. "I spoke with Lloyd at Thistle and Thatch, and he assured me this is a true antique. He said you might know of others who own figurines like this."

"I don't believe so. Many people have similar figurines to this one, but not necessarily antique ones. You can get cheaper versions in almost any gift shop in the UK. However, I can tell this is the real thing." She turned it over to examine the base. Suddenly, she sat up straight. She threw Harriet a puzzled glance, her usual smile gone. "Where did you say this came from?"

Harriet repeated, "It was a gift." She grew alert with curiosity when she saw a troubled expression creep over Jane's face. "Why? Do you recognize it?"

"Indeed I do." Jane gave a curt dip of her chin. "It belongs to me."

It was Harriet's turn to frown. "It belongs to you? Are you sure?"

Jane pointed to the fireplace mantel. "That's its mate over there." She pointed to the tiny red dot on the bottom of the figurine's base. "Do you see this red speck? My mother put it there."

She handed the porcelain dog back to Harriet then rose and retrieved the matching dog from the mantel. She presented it to Harriet upside down. "See? Another red dot of my mother's fingernail polish. She marked them years ago when I was an infant, during the war."

Harriet felt an uptick in her pulse. Had she been wrong about Randy? Had he stolen the dog from Jane Birtwhistle after all? Or perhaps his friend Gabriel was the thief? With a hint of dread in her tone, she asked Jane, "So the little dog was stolen from you?"

Jane cocked her head to one side. "Not necessarily." She refilled her teacup and gestured toward Harriet's. "Another cuppa?"

Harriet shook her head. The slight lump in her throat assured her that she wouldn't be able to swallow a drop. "I'm not sure I understand."

"It's a rather long story," Jane said, after taking a sip. "The fact of the matter is that this particular figurine has been missing for years. Along with others like it."

"I'm in no hurry," Harriet assured her. "I'd like to hear the whole story."

"I'll be right back. There's something I want to show you." Jane left the room and returned with an old canvas-covered book, which looked like a journal of some sort. She handed it to Harriet, who opened it.

"Florence Birtwhistle?" she asked, noting the name inside the front page.

"My mother," Jane explained. "This is her journal. It details everything I'm about to explain to you. During World War II, my father served in France and my mother lived in this very cottage with her widowed father. There was a great deal of anxiety over a possible Nazi invasion. The villagers feared the Nazis would plunder the family heirlooms and treasures belonging to the residents. She wrote all about it there in her wartime journal."

Harriet nodded. "The Nazis did that throughout Europe—stealing and plundering."

"Yes, it was a well-founded concern," Jane agreed. "These figurines were precious to Mum because they had belonged to her mother and her grandmother before that. So, she packed them up and a few other things and hid them away to keep them from falling into Nazi hands. Leery of "putting all her eggs in one basket," as she said in that journal, she separated the pairs, putting half in a crate and the other half in an old sea chest her father had. Then my grandfather hid the chest and the crate in different locations. She kept a few here at home because they were her favorites, but their mates were put away for safekeeping."

"That seems like a sensible thing to do," Harriet said.

"Mum put a dab of color on the bottom of each piece so she would know which figurines were hers and listed them in her journal—just in case. Staffordshire china was popular in the region, and she was afraid the figurines might get mixed in with someone else's. Apparently, people all over the village did the same—hid their valuables in nooks and crannies of the church, in the old smugglers' caves and tunnels, and some in family crypts."

Harriet listened, intrigued. She turned her attention to the figurines. "And then your mother retrieved her valuables from their hiding place after the war?"

"No. Mum had her hands full nursing my father back to health. He wasn't quite himself after the war. He was weak and depressed, suffering from what they called shell shock."

"Yes, though now they call it post-traumatic stress disorder," Harriet said. "It's a very serious condition."

"That's right. It was difficult for people to recover from the war. Rationing remained in effect for years afterward. Most people seemed overwhelmed with the loss of so many brothers, sons, and husbands. The soldiers who returned were barely recognizable as the ones who'd left. Retrieving family heirlooms was not a high priority at first. People were too busy trying to pick up the pieces of their lives."

"So she never recovered the crate or the sea chest?"

"Not that I'm aware of." Jane indicated Harriet's dog figurine. "And that would have been in one them."

Harriet seemed perplexed. "Did she forget about them?"

"Actually, Mum didn't know where exactly they'd been stashed. Her father, John Woodley, hid them somewhere, presumably in one of the old smugglers' tunnels. The town is riddled with them, you know. He had a stroke not long after the war ended and never fully recovered his ability to speak. At least, that's what Mum wrote in her journal. Neither the crate nor the chest was ever recovered, because only he knew where they were."

Harriet sat silent for a while, trying to absorb what Jane had shared with her. Finally, she said, "I don't quite understand. It's been decades since the war ended. Surely someone would have found them by now and returned them to your family. Was your mother's name on the outside of the crate or the chest?"

"It was," Jane said. "Mum and I always assumed that someone found them and kept the contents for themselves. Times were hard. They might have sold the figurines for cash to help them get by. Or maybe they were never found." She indicated the little dog again. "Except that now it seems that the crate or the sea chest was found, or maybe both. Do you know when or where this little dog was found?"

"Unfortunately, I don't. I don't even know where the person who gave it to me got it—whether they found it or purchased it from a rummage sale or what," Harriet admitted. She held the figurine out to Jane. "You keep it. It rightfully belongs to you."

"But it was given to you as a gift," Jane protested, even as she accepted the little dog.

"Yes, and I will do all I can to discover where it came from. I should have asked more questions at the time."

Harriet realized with some misgivings that she would need to have a heart-to-heart talk with Doreen and Randy. The figurine was valuable and belonged to Jane. If the boy had obtained it somehow, did he also have the other missing figurines in his possession? Had he found the crate or seaman's chest in a smugglers' tunnel?

Jane placed her cup and saucer on the table, pushing away an orange cat trying to help himself to the cream. "It's possible that everything my mum packed away—except for this dog figurine—has been smashed to smithereens somewhere. She often supposed that might have happened, depending on where my grandfather hid them. The collapse of an old tunnel, the crumbling of a wall." She held the porcelain figurine close. "This might be the only one that survived intact."

"I certainly intend to find out," Harriet said. It was possible, she supposed, that the figurines had been recovered years ago and kept by the person who found them. Now someone in that family had held a rummage sale to get rid of things in the attic. She handed the journal back to Jane, wishing she had time to read it from cover to cover.

"I won't press you to tell me who gave you the dog as a gift," Jane said. She placed the faded journal on her lap. "But it would mean a great deal to me to have the items restored if possible. They are family heirlooms. While they do have monetary value, for me, it's the sentimental value that's most important. I have no family left—no siblings or children of my own. I never married, you know." She gave a wistful smile.

"I know." Harriet reached over to squeeze the elderly woman's delicate hand. Then she rose, careful not to step on the calico cat curled up at her feet. "I'll see what I can do about finding any others. They all have the little red mark on the bottom, right?"

Jane rose too. "Yes, they should all be marked with that pinpoint of nail polish."

"And you're sure she doesn't mention in her journal where the items were hidden?" Harriet asked.

"She doesn't. I'm sure she didn't know," Jane said.

"Well, don't give up on more of the figurines being found. It's possible, as you say, that someone found either the chest or the crate long ago and the figurines are now being sold off at a rummage sale or in a thrift shop."

Jane's face lit up with hope. "Yes, it is possible."

Carefully making her way to the door so as not to step on a cat, Harriet sent up a silent prayer that Randy had indeed found the figurine in a secondhand store or at a flea market. Perhaps he'd even found it in an old tunnel somewhere or maybe a cave. There were certainly plenty of those around.

After saying her goodbyes, Harriet made her way to the old Land Rover she'd inherited from her grandfather, a thousand thoughts flickering through her mind. Rummage sales, flea markets, thrift shops, caves, and tunnels. Attics even. The possibilities were endless. She needed to find out where Randy had come by the little porcelain dog.

She picked up the groceries on her short list and returned home, still thinking of how to tactfully question Randy.

She'd barely parked her car in its designated space when her cell phone rang. It was Will. She answered, her mind still on porcelain figurines. "Hello, my dear. How are you?"

"Harriet, I found another one." He sounded slightly exasperated.

She swallowed hard as she realized what he meant. "Another bat in the belfry?"

"I'm afraid so."

She let out a long breath. "Oh dear."

CHAPTER THIRTEEN

Harriet found herself so distracted on Sunday morning that she could hardly concentrate on the church service. Although Will's sermon was eloquent and insightful, as usual, she found herself peering up at the rafters in the high ceiling of the sanctuary, wondering if more and more bats would continue to fly into the belfry. She could almost imagine the creatures swooping down among the unsuspecting congregation.

It was all nonsense, of course. She was letting her imagination run rampant. Bats were shy, nocturnal creatures and not aggressive at all, although they could become quite defensive if handled. She'd learned a lot about them in her research. After Will told her he'd found another one on the floor in the belfry, she'd revisited the Bat Conservation Trust website.

This time, she'd also called the bat helpline. With two bats now, the situation felt more urgent. Fortunately, she was able to reach someone. A volunteer named Neville Branson said he would come for the bats on Monday. He advised her to give them fresh water once or twice a day and to put a dishcloth in the birdcage so they could stay warm. He seemed quite pleased when she told him she'd been doing that already.

She was reassured to learn that rabies was the only known disease found in UK bats that could be transmitted to humans.

Fortunately, the risk of this happening was quite small, Mr. Branson assured her. Harriet heaved a sigh of relief when she learned that no cases of bats infecting household pets had been reported either. That meant she didn't need to worry about Charlie and Maxwell contracting a virus from a bat. Nor were any of her animal patients at risk.

Harriet had made a few notes, realizing as she did so that bats were far more interesting creatures than she'd first thought. A bat that bared its teeth in a fierce manner, for instance, was actually using its unique form of echolocation—a sort of sonar inaudible to most humans—to scan its environment for "information." She marveled as she learned more about the vital role bats played in ecosystems around the world. If Randy and Gabriel came by to see the bats, she'd share these interesting facts with them too. Maybe it would give them a better appreciation for the unusual animals.

Jolted out of her reverie by those around her standing to sing a hymn, Harriet rose to her feet and forced herself to quit thinking about bats. Instead, she tried to concentrate on the remainder of the service. She'd noticed Doreen and the rest of the Danby family filling their usual pew—the kids scrubbed clean, their hair brushed and tidy. Little Terrance, now a perky six-year-old, was especially cute in his blue Oxford shirt buttoned all the way to the top.

As soon as the service was over and the final "Amen" repeated, most people lingered in the fellowship hall to enjoy a spot of tea. Harriet made a point of intercepting her friend as soon as she was able. "Doreen, can I speak with you in private? It's rather important."

"Of course." Doreen scanned the crowd of chatting parishioners. "Don't know where we can go for a private word though. What did you have in mind?"

"The cemetery," Harriet suggested.

Doreen laughed. "Lead the way." She shooed her husband, Tom, and the children off to have tea and then followed Harriet outside.

It was one of those perfect summer days—the sort Harriet wished could be saved in a jar and released at some later time when the weather was foul and gloomy. The sun was warm but not stifling. Flowers released their sweet fragrance. Even in a cemetery, the day felt optimistic and fresh. The fluffy clouds against the deep blue sky overhead reminded her of dollops of whipped cream.

"I'm hungrier than I thought," she said with a chuckle.

"What's that?" Doreen asked.

Harriet grinned. "Nothing. Just talking to myself."

Doreen shook her head. The hint of a smile twitched the corners of her mouth. "They say that's a bad sign, Harriet. Maybe I should start worrying about you."

"You probably should," Harriet quipped. Then she grew serious. "Have you had time to speak with Randy about the dog figurine?"

"I have," Doreen said, skirting a large headstone in the shape of a Celtic cross. "I couldn't get a straight answer out of him though. He insists he found it in a box of old rubbish. He cleaned it up and gave it to you as a present. That's what he told me."

"Do you believe him?" Harriet asked quietly. She hoped she hadn't offended her friend by insinuating that her son might have lied to her. She cared for Doreen deeply and wouldn't willingly hurt her feelings for the world.

"I do believe him." Doreen hesitated for a moment before adding, "And yet, I'm not sure he's telling me the entire truth. Do you know what I mean?"

"I think so," Harriet replied. "He's leaving something out, right? Something like where he found the box of rubbish."

Doreen eyed her. "Have you learned something about all of this?"

"I have. The figurine belongs to Jane Birtwhistle. I'd really like to know all the details, anything more specific Randy can tell me. So would Jane."

Doreen gasped, her gray eyes widening with disbelief. "You say it actually belongs to Jane? What did you do with it?"

"I gave it to her yesterday. She was so grateful to have it returned. It's part of a matching pair. Apparently, she's missing several little figurines that were in her family for generations, going back to her great-grandmother. They're beloved family heirlooms." Harriet went on to summarize what she'd learned from Jane regarding her mother's efforts to hide the family's valuables during World War II.

At first, Doreen seemed speechless. It was so quiet in the cemetery that Harriet became aware of the gentle twittering of the birds. She felt her cheeks grow warm with embarrassment. It wasn't an easy thing to practically accuse a friend's child of perhaps lying and stealing. But she couldn't believe Randy was guilty of either, and the best way to prove that was to get the truth from him.

"There has to be an explanation. There just has to be," Harriet went on. "Jane said the dog figurine and the others have been missing for decades. We need to find out where Randy found that box."

Finally, Doreen asked in a tight voice, "Did you tell Jane where the porcelain dog came from?"

"No, I didn't," Harriet said. "I just told her I'd received it as a gift. She didn't press for details or an explanation. She seemed to understand I wanted to keep that private."

"And she's certain it's hers?" Doreen paused in front of another marker, this one engraved with an angel's profile.

"Yes, and she has proof." As Harriet stood next to Doreen, she went on to explain about the nail polish and how the figurines were divided into two boxes and hidden separately.

"It doesn't make sense. How could Randy find something like that?" Doreen asked. "The war was a long time ago. Someone must have found those pieces before now."

"It's possible that someone did and kept the contents, but now they or their descendants are selling off their old knickknacks. Randy may be telling the truth that he found the figurine—perhaps in a rummage sale or a thrift shop. He told you it was in a box of junk, right? Well, that fits with rummage sales and even some thrift stores. Sometimes you can buy a whole box of stuff for a small amount of money. It's like a mystery grab bag. Those are always popular with kids."

Doreen fell silent as they reached the oldest section of the cemetery.

Harriet broke the silence. "Would you let me speak with Randy? Perhaps he'd be more open, more specific with me. After all, I can't ground him."

"It's okay with me," Doreen said. "But I still can't help thinking that Gabriel Mellon is involved in this somehow. Maybe Randy is keeping mum about the details because if he talks, Gabriel might get angry with him. Gabriel's grandmother lives in the village, in an old house near the shore. Maybe the boys have been digging through her attic or something. That could explain why Randy's being cagey."

"Speaking of Gabriel, I saw him biking with Randy yesterday. They were headed to your place. I stopped, and we had a word or two. I invited the boys to come see the bat. You should let Randy know I now have two."

"Tom put them both to work mending a fence," Doreen said. "Gabriel stayed for supper too. I was too harsh on the boy, Harriet. There's some good in him. I saw that by the way he treated Terrance."

Harriet slipped her arm around her friend's shoulders, giving her a hug. "Maybe Randy and your family will be a good influence on him."

Doreen snorted. "As long as it's not the other way around. Ava sat at the table last night making sheep's eyes at him. To his credit, he didn't seem to encourage her. He was more interested in Terrance's pet turtle." She shook her head.

"I don't want you to worry about the figurine. I'll get to the bottom of it," Harriet assured her. "But please don't mention to Randy that I want a private chat with him. I don't want him to avoid me. I'll approach him when the time is right. Maybe I can take him out for ice cream or something, just the two of us."

"Good luck prying him away from Gabriel," Doreen said wryly.

Harriet grinned. "Leave that to me."

"And it you're in the mood to play good auntie, you can have a talk with Ava too—talk some sense into that girl." Together, they started back toward the fellowship hall. "She's been acting a bit squirrelly lately."

"Because of Gabriel?" Harriet asked.

Doreen shrugged. "She does have a crush on him, but there's something else going on too. I can't put my finger on it. It's like she's keeping a secret. Sometimes she seems worried, and the next minute she's happy as a clam. And the other day Randy started to say something and she shushed him and then looked at me. But she's not talking about it, whatever it is."

"It sounds like the three of them are up to something," Harriet suggested.

"That's it exactly," Doreen replied. "But I can't pry a word out of them."

They returned to the fellowship hall, where Doreen reunited with her husband. Together they rounded up their brood and headed home. Harriet stepped aside to make a call. She hadn't forgotten that it was Father's Day in the US. She'd figured out the time difference between White Church Bay and Connecticut and decided it was early, but not too early, to call her father. He'd been a morning person for as long as she could remember.

As she expected, he picked up right away, clearly overjoyed to hear from her. Harriet chatted with him while she waited for Will to finish his pastoral duties and change into more comfortable clothes.

Polly approached her with a small, elderly woman clinging to her arm. "Harriet, I want you to meet my grandmother, Callista Thatcher. Gran, this is Dr. Harriet Bailey. I work for her now."

Callista shook Harriet's hand with a firm grip. "I remember your grandfather. Good man. Dabbled with paints, as I recall. Waste of time, in my opinion, but it seemed to make him happy."

Harriet and Polly exchanged glances. A waste of time? Harriet let the comment slide.

With eyes narrowed and voice low, Callista added, "I hear you're something of a sleuth in your spare time. If so, you might want to keep an eye on that odd pair staying at the Quill and Scroll. Seen 'em around town, I have. Peering here and there with their binoculars."

Harriet smiled. "I understand they're bird-watching."

"Bird-watching, ha! So they say. Why are they looking into people's windows then?"

"You actually saw them looking in your window?" Harriet asked.

Callista's expression grew even more sour. "Didn't say it was my window, did I?"

Before Harriet could respond, Polly's grandmother gave a snort and teetered away to speak with someone else.

Polly raised her eyebrows. "Sorry about that, Harriet. What can I say? She's a grumpy old thing. I warned you."

"You did," Harriet agreed with a smile. "But I'm glad to meet her, all the same."

Polly looked over Harriet's shoulder. "Oh, no. She's cornered Jane Birtwhistle. I'd better go save poor Jane." Polly hurried after her grandmother.

Harriet watched her retreating figure. Now that she'd met Polly's grandmother in person, she was inclined to write off the elderly woman's suspicions as unfounded. Whose window might the Clutterbucks have been looking into? And for what reason? Harriet thought it more likely to be the assumption of a paranoid old woman.

Will soon joined her, and they drove to Aunt Jinny's, who was expecting them for lunch. Harriet's cousin, Anthony, and his family wouldn't be there, as they were enjoying a family vacation in the British Virgin Islands.

However, she was pleasantly surprised when Polly and Van joined them. One never knew who might show up on a Sunday afternoon at her aunt's dining table. Aunt Jinny was always inviting friends and neighbors. Polly's eyes sparkled and her cheeks glowed, just as they always did whenever she was with Van. Van looked happy too, gazing at Polly when she spoke, as if she were a heavenly messenger.

"Something smells divine," Harriet said, sniffing appreciatively.

"Then let's eat. The food is ready." Aunt Jinny ushered everyone to the table. "Pastor, will you say grace?"

After he obliged, they wasted no time in filling their plates. As usual, Aunt Jinny had outdone herself. The succulent roast chicken was surrounded by carrots, potatoes, and onions. Harriet took an extra portion of wild rice studded with mushrooms, settling it beside aromatic grilled asparagus.

In between bites, Van said to Harriet, "Sergeant Oduba and I went to the Quill and Scroll to have a look around. Glad you gave me the heads up about the strange sounds Mrs. Beem was complaining about."

Harriet paused with a forkful of chicken halfway to her mouth. "Did you find something?"

"Indeed we did."

"And you arrested the ghost for disturbing the peace," Aunt Jinny joked.

Everyone laughed.

Van said, "We've made an arrest, and it wasn't a ghost." He briefly explained about the car part thieves, adding, "When we took possession of the stolen goods, there didn't seem to be as many as we'd expected. Come to find out they'd hidden the rest of the loot behind the Quill and Scroll, on the Beems' property. I imagine that's what Mrs. Beem has been hearing."

"Isn't it wonderful?" Polly exclaimed. "Now that poor couple won't have to worry about strange noises scaring their customers—or them." She beamed at Van with open pride. "Great work, Van."

Van flushed and ducked his head. "Just doing my job."

Will scooped up some wild rice. "So you think the thieves made all the racket as they hid the car parts."

"Yes." Van took a sip of water. "Can't think what else those noises could be."

Harriet frowned. "I'm confused. Did they hide the stolen goods in the cellar at the inn?"

"No, we found them outside near the back wall, behind some bushes and a stack of unused lumber left over from the renovation," Van old her.

Harriet felt vaguely dissatisfied, even as she continued to eat Aunt Jinny's delicious food. She supposed noise from outside could be heard in the parlor. But was it likely? Besides, Celia had told them she'd heard the noises in the daytime, not at night. Would the thieves risk stashing stolen goods on the inn property in broad daylight?

"I'm sure the Beems feel greatly relieved now that you've gotten to the bottom of things," Will said with an approving nod. "Congratulations, Detective Constable, on a job well done."

Van flushed again as he accepted the basket of yeast rolls Aunt Jinny passed to him.

Harriet's cell phone jingled. She excused herself from the table and went to answer it in the living room. It might be an animal emergency. Friends and family understood that she was always on call. She just hoped it wasn't anything too serious.

But it wasn't an animal emergency. "Harriet, it's Celia. Can you come to the inn right away? We're in the parlor, and we hear voices." Harriet thought she heard a sob behind the words. "Please say you'll come. Please."

CHAPTER FOURTEEN

White Church Bay
June 1941

Flory continued to listen as Marietta shared her idea.

"As I said, it would be daft to hide all our valuables in one place. Those Nazis have already bombed Bridlington, Hornsea, and a few of the RAF airfields in Yorkshire, so we mustn't suppose we'll escape their attention here in the Bay."

Flory's heart sank as she realized her friend was right.

"Why, Mavis White's boys have been playing air raid and practicing bandaging one another up in case there are civilian casualties. Others ride their bicycles out near the fields when they see an aeroplane, hoping they'll be the first to spot a German parachuting from the sky. Everyone's taking first aid courses, and there's supposed to be a lecture on emergency childbirth procedures at the town hall next week. I'm planning on going."

Shaken and troubled, Flory remained silent. She agreed with everything her friend was saying—they needed to take precautions. It saddened her to think of White Church Bay becoming a heap of rubble in the wake of a bombing by the enemy. She'd seen the photos in the newspaper of youngsters in London and Coventry playing amid piles of brick, shattered lumber, and even smoldering debris. It wasn't what she wanted for Jane, but if she'd learned anything over the past couple of years, it was that she might not have a choice.

"So you see," Marietta continued, pushing away her empty bowl, "one of those rockets might destroy our homes. That's why we need to have our valuables safe and away, just as Miss Dingle said. We have to protect what's important to us, and we might also need to make sure we have something to rebuild with if we need it."

"But where? Besides the old smugglers' tunnels, I mean?" Flory asked. "Surely the tunnels aren't big enough to accommodate everyone's belongings."

Marietta waved a dismissive hand. "I doubt everyone will do what we're planning to. Mavis has permission from the vicar to hide a small trunk at the church. There are all sorts of vaults and hidey-holes from the old days, even in the belfry. A few crypts too. The parish records and other valuables have already been stashed away, including some communion wine and wafers, as well as a small wireless. The vicar said radios would be confiscated if the Nazis invade, and the village would need at least one in case of emergencies."

Flory frowned. "But the Nazis might bomb the church."

"True, but the vaults are underground. It's hoped the things stashed there will remain hidden and intact. So what do you say, Flory? Want to divide your valuables into two crates? We'll hide one at the church and one in the tunnel Miss Dingle recommended."

"I'm for it," Flory agreed. Why shouldn't she be? "I think the precaution would please Dad. He seemed none too confident that the old caves and passageways would be able to sustain a heavy bombing. The walls are old, and he's concerned about the stability. Where are these secret tunnels anyway?" She envisioned musty, rodent-infested cellars. She'd heard about them all her life growing up in the village. But not being an adventurous sort, she had never ventured into one.

"All around town near the shore, or so I've heard," Marietta said. "I've never seen one myself. Simon told me that some of the old houses along the beach are connected by secret passageways. Supposedly, that was to ensure that stolen goods could be secretly moved from one house to another. He and his brothers used to explore them when they were boys. There are a few caves too, with secret hiding places. If you and I have lived here all our lives and don't know where they are, I don't see how the Nazis could ever find them."

"Is Simon on patrol tonight?" Flory asked.

"Yes, Simon is on patrol."

"He must be worn to the bone." Simon had to be up before dawn to collect the milk from the dairy farmers and make deliveries in the village.

Marietta heaved a sigh. "He is, and none too happy about it either. He's willing to do his part, but he says the Home Guard isn't equipped to fight the Germans when they get here. They only have broomsticks and whatever they can scrounge up at home to drill with. Fat lot of good those will do on invasion day against guns and whatnot."

"Yes, Dad gets down in the mouth about it sometimes. Not about patrolling, I mean, but not having weapons and the like."

With a snort, Marietta replied, "And without cartridges, those old guns are useless too. Did you hear about the boys over in Whitby who practice lobbing grenades? They've swiped all the brass bed knobs they can find to use as substitutes." She chuckled. "You have to admire their effort, but who do they think is going to supply them with the real thing?"

Flory slumped in her chair. "Sometimes I feel guilty I'm not doing more for the war effort."

"How can you say that?" Marietta straightened her shoulders. "You're doing your part. We all are. Why, we're fighting battles of a different sort every day right in our own kitchens."

With a sigh, Flory acknowledged the truth of it.

Leaning forward, Marietta added, "I know you've seen the posters declaring 'Food is a munition of war. Don't waste it.'"

Yes, Flory had seen the posters. No one wasted food anymore. They hadn't even thrown rice at Sharon Merritt's wedding. The vicar's wife had suggested that those attending give packets of rice as wedding presents instead. Wanting to keep some tradition for the event, Sharon's mother and several of her friends had gathered scraps of paper, which they cut into small bits to use as confetti.

"I spend a lot of time organizing our ration coupons and experimenting in the kitchen, trying to make sure Dad still has nice things to eat," Flory said. "Last month I even managed a birthday cake for him using flour, custard powder, and dried eggs. He enjoyed it—or at least he said he did."

"I'm sure he relished every bite," Marietta said encouragingly. "I tried making lentil cutlets one night." She gave a dry chuckle. "Simon said he'd rather have a plate piled with boiled potatoes and margarine. I can't say I blame him."

"Listen to Dr. Carrot and Potato Pete," Flory teased. She was referring to the potato and carrot figures used in ads to remind British citizens that they had other food options available besides the ones that were rationed. "They're always offering suggestions in magazines and newspapers for new recipes."

"Yes, I tried the carrot flan recipe." Marietta wrinkled her nose. "I don't recommend it."

Hearing a whimper, Flory rose from her chair and hurried to the bedroom. She returned to the kitchen with a yawning Jane cradled in her arms.

"There's that sweet angel," Marietta cooed. "May I hold her?" She shifted in her chair and held out her arms.

"Of course." Flory carefully passed Jane to her friend. Even in such dark times, she knew how babies could cheer those around them. It was something about the innocence in their eyes. They were as yet untouched by war, and they made adults want to keep it that way.

"You'll be wanting to hide those porcelain figurines that belonged to your mum," Marietta murmured. She made a face at Jane, and the baby giggled.

Flory glanced absently toward the sitting room where her mother's collection of Staffordshire figurines stood. "I've been thinking that myself. My mother and grandmother kept them safe in the last world war. Now it's my duty to do the same."

"Then divide the collection in half," Marietta advised. "Put half in one crate and the other half in another container. That way, even if something happens to one of the crates, the other will be safe. It's much less likely that someone will be able to take or destroy the whole collection if it's not all together. What else are you going to hide?"

"Other than Mum's figurines, I'm not sure what else I have of any value," Flory said. "My family has always had what we needed, but not much more than that."

"I mean, I don't expect you to need to hide family portraits, rare paintings, and silver like Lord Beresford, but make sure you're thinking outside the box. There are many in town who have valuable jewelry. Miss Dingle has a coin collection that belonged to her father. She says it's worth a pretty penny." Marietta's mouth twisted into a grin. "Get it?"

Flory groaned. "They should ration your jokes next."

Marietta lifted her chin. "They can try."

The women laughed together.

"Some of the ladies at the meeting suggested hiding tinned goods," Flory said, getting back to the matter at hand. "What do you think?"

Marietta replied breezily, "Simon and I aren't going to do that, but I'll admit we've been putting by as much extra as we can spare for quite a while now. Tinned soup and salmon, powdered milk, dried lentils, oats and dried yeast, even candles and matches. We've been buying American tinned meat too. Just in case. Apparently, that stuff can last for years if it's stored properly."

Flory nodded, suddenly feeling the weight of the world on her shoulders. With some hesitation, she asked, "You're not buying the extra food on the black market, are you?"

Everything from nappies to perfume, sugar, and soap was available if one knew where to look. Despite the government's best efforts to stamp out the black market, it seemed to be thriving. Flory didn't even know how one would go about purchasing items that way. She imagined sleazy characters in low-brimmed hats hanging around in pubs, tempting their fellows with hard-to-find items, even though it was against the law—not to mention unpatriotic. It undermined the whole point of rationing.

"Not at all. We're simply using our coupons wisely and doing a bit of bartering now and then. As frustrating and confusing as the regulations are, I spend a lot of time keeping up with the changes and hunting for sales where I can find them. I must say, I'm getter bolder by the day too. I would never have accosted a stranger on the street a year ago, but just last week, I saw a young woman with two onions in her string bag and I almost knocked her down in my eagerness to discover where she'd purchased them."

Flory laughed, picturing it. "I've done the same myself. Walked right up to a woman I'd never spoken to in my life and said, 'Ma'am, where did you get that rutabaga?' Fortunately, everyone seems to understand, so they're all quite willing to tell you." And in light of that, the world didn't feel so heavy on her shoulders. After all, there were other shoulders sharing the load.

They laughed again, and then Marietta rose, handing the baby to Flory. "I think the rain is letting up, so I'd better be off. Thanks for the soup. I'll bring by some of mine sometime to pay you back."

"That's not necessary," Flory protested. "You always share what you have with me."

Marietta met her gaze squarely. "How many times must I remind you that you need it? It's on you to keep your little one hale and hearty. I'll hear no more about it."

Flory smiled. "Thank you, Marietta. You always know how to lift my spirits."

"And you mine. We had supper earlier with Simon's mum. She served rabbit stew. The gravy was thin and gray with little bones floating in it. There was stewed rhubarb without sugar for dessert. Mrs. Trumble did her best, but Simon was not pleased."

"I don't imagine he was." Flory followed Marietta to the door and watched as her friend slipped on her coat and covered her head with a scarf. "Be careful. It's awfully dark out tonight. You don't want to take a tumble."

Marietta gave her a one-armed hug, careful not to jostle the baby in Flory's arms. "Don't worry about me. I've got great night vision—must be all those carrots I've been eating."

"Carrot flan," Flory threw in.

"And carrot cake," Marietta added. "Good thing desserts are now healthy."

"Not to mention carrot cutlets and carrot curry," Flory joked.

Marietta stepped out into the damp night, still laughing.

And even though the world outside was dark and Flory still hadn't lit so much as a candle, the visit from her friend left the cottage feeling a little brighter than it had been before.

CHAPTER FIFTEEN

"I must go," Harriet apologized. She kissed Aunt Jinny on the cheek. "Thank you for the lovely meal. I'm sorry to eat and run, but Celia Beem is hearing things in the parlor again. As you can imagine, she's beside herself after thinking that was all over. I really want to help her if I can. And this time, I might actually hear the strange noises for myself."

"I understand," her aunt said, rising. "I'm glad you at least got to eat some dinner."

Van stood as well, laying his napkin beside his plate. "I think I'd better go too. After Sergeant Oduba and I rounded up the perpetrators and took possession of the stolen goods, I thought the strange noises at the inn would come to an end. But it seems something else is afoot."

"I want to come too," Polly insisted, scrambling for her purse. "What if there's more loot hidden on the Beems' property and other thieves have come to collect it? They're a bold lot, aren't they? Trespassing in broad daylight. Or maybe it really is a ghost or a prankster." She gave them a mischievous grin.

"I suppose that's possible," Van acknowledged. "A prankster, I mean. Not the ghost thing."

With an apologetic smile for Aunt Jinny, Will also rose and pushed in his chair. "I think I'd better go along too and take a second look at that cellar. Seems to me there must be a secret passageway or hidden entrance that someone has access to. We didn't find anything the first time, but perhaps we didn't look hard enough." Reaching for Harriet's hand, Will added, "The meal was delicious, Jinny. Thank you so much."

"You're more than welcome," Aunt Jinny assured him with a gracious smile.

"I can come back later to help with the cleanup," Harriet added.

"I will too," Polly chimed in.

Aunt Jinny flapped a hand. "Nonsense. Go on with you now. Just make sure one of you tells me all about it later. I'm as curious as can be. I'm only sorry that you don't have time to eat the blueberry buckle I made for dessert." She sighed in an exaggerated way. "I guess I'll have to eat it all by myself."

"You're a dear," Harriet said. She gave her aunt another peck on the cheek and bustled out the door.

"I'll drive," Will told Harriet as they hurried out to the parking area. "I hate abandoning your aunt with all the dishes."

"She understands," Harriet assured him. "And we'll make it up to her later. For now, duty calls." She waved at Polly and Van, who intended to follow them to the inn.

"Jinny is a remarkable woman," Will said, opening the passenger door for Harriet. "Rather like her niece."

Harriet kissed his cheek then climbed into the car. She silently thanked the Lord for sending this man into her life—a rather remarkable man in his own right.

As they drove toward the village, Harriet took the time to admire the sunny buttercups on the side of the road and the purple thistles. What a beautiful place she lived in. She felt a rush of gratitude for her grandad, who had inspired her to become a veterinarian in the first place then left her a beautiful home and thriving business. He'd always put his family first, even when he wasn't around to see the results.

It wasn't a long drive to the inn, and soon Harriet, Will, Polly, and Van were at the front door.

Before they could knock, Freddie opened it, looking rather flustered and slightly embarrassed. His red hair stuck out here and there as if he'd run his fingers through it more than once. "Thanks for coming on such short notice. So sorry for the bother," he apologized. "I told Celia not to call, but she insisted. She's in a bad way." He raised an eyebrow when he recognized Van. "But surely you didn't need to bring the police."

"The four of us were dining together at my aunt's home when your wife called, so Van's not here in an official capacity," Harriet explained, even as she wondered whether they had overreacted by arriving in force. "You already know DC Van Worthington, of course, and this is my receptionist, Polly Thatcher."

"Nice to meet you," Polly said, her gaze traveling around the inn's attractive interior. Harriet recognized the gleam in Polly's eyes. Her best friend was hoping to hear the ghostly noises for herself.

Harriet couldn't blame her. She wanted to hear them as well.

"Did *you* hear anything out of the ordinary this time?" Harriet asked. "Or just Celia?"

Freddie shook his head. "I didn't hear a thing. However, two of our guests were in the parlor at the time. Celia was bringing them some tea. They said they'd heard the voices too. They're in there with her now. Follow me. Maybe you'll hear something for yourselves. This is really getting to my wife. I'd like to get to the bottom of it."

To Harriet's surprise, the two guests Freddie had mentioned proved to be the Clutterbuck brothers. The men moved about the parlor tapping the walls, likely listening for a hollow place. She cast a sympathetic glance at Celia, who slumped in discouragement on the storage bench.

Harriet approached her and laid a hand on her shoulder. "What sort of voices did you hear this time?"

"Soft murmuring voices. Again." Celia's tone was weary and discouraged. Her face was drawn and pale.

"Sounded to me like it was coming from there," said one of the twins. He pointed to the bench where Celia sat.

Freddie stepped forward to make introductions. "These are our guests—Michael and Matthew Clutterbuck. They're here adding shorebirds to their life lists."

"Life list?" Van echoed, puzzled.

"The record of all the birds we've seen and identified. We're twitchers. Bird watchers," the other twin explained. Harriet wasn't sure if he was Michael or Matthew. Freddie had introduced the brothers as a pair.

Callista Thatcher's suspicions about the twins rang in her mind. Harriet, however, was inclined to believe the men had nothing to do with the strange noises plaguing Celia's peace of mind. After all, here they were, tapping the walls and trying to help Celia discover what was going on. They were likely what they claimed to be—out-of-town visitors adding new birds to their life lists.

Still, she might suggest that Van do a background check on them, just to be on the safe side.

Will nudged Van. "Let's check out the cellar again."

Van agreed, and Freddie volunteered to go with them.

When the men left the parlor with Freddie leading the way and grumbling something about pranks having gone on long enough, Harriet turned to the twins. "You heard the voices too just now?"

One of them—was it Michael or Matthew?—gave a curt nod. "Indeed. Faint voices. Couldn't even distinguish if they were male or female. But someone is prowling about. Must be. No other explanation. Some pranksters, I daresay. Couldn't be prowlers, could it? I mean, not on a Sunday afternoon."

"Sort of whispery voices," the other brother added.

Harriet regarded the twins thoughtfully. They were with Celia when she'd heard the voices, so they couldn't have made the sounds themselves, or Celia would have noticed. Again, she wondered if she should scratch the two men off her list of suspects. They might be guilty of peeping into other people's windows—if Polly's grandmother was to be believed—but did that mean they were responsible for plaguing Celia with unidentifiable noises?

Harriet motioned for Celia to get up off the bench. When she did, Harriet tugged on it, but no pulling or poking or tugging caused the bench to budge. She'd hoped it would scrape across the floor and reveal a hidden passageway. It didn't.

"We tried that already," Celia told her. "The bench is built into the wall."

"Do you keep anything inside it?" Polly asked.

"Odds and ends. Nothing important," Celia replied.

Harriet lifted the lid. There was nothing inside but some magazines, a street map of the town, and an old telephone directory with curled pages, yellow with age. Disappointed, she lowered the lid again. "Polly, let's have a look around outside."

"We'll come along, shall we?" one of the brothers offered. "We've heard about pirates and smugglers along these shores. Think there are modern-day smugglers about? That would be an adventure to tumble into."

Harriet and Polly exchanged a glance. There had indeed been recent smuggling activity in the bay. Harriet thought it best not to mention the criminals who'd used lobster traps to steal antiquities.

"More exciting than bird-watching, I imagine," Harriet said, smiling at the brothers.

They returned her smile. "Close to it, anyway."

Celia led them to the kitchen and opened the back door, allowing them access to the outside property. The Clutterbucks moved with quick, jerky steps as the group walked the perimeter, looking for anything out of the ordinary. Harriet and Polly followed closely behind, but Harriet didn't see anything to attract her attention. Nor did she hear anything. Along the stone walls, she noted that the old coal chute had been sealed and there didn't seem to be any secret doors or hidden entrances.

"I think this so-called haunting or harassment or whatever you want to call it has gone on long enough," Polly declared, a spark of anger in her eyes. "Someone is going to a lot of trouble trying to scare the Beems into leaving town or at least closing their business. I can't think of any other explanation."

"Is that what this is all about?" one of the men asked.

"I'm not sure what's going on," Harriet said. "But I intend to get to the bottom of it."

"You don't think it could be a ghost, do you?" the other asked politely.

Harriet arched an eyebrow. "Do you believe in ghosts, Mr. Clutterbuck?"

"Truth be told, I've never given it much thought. What say you, Michael?"

Michael frowned pensively. His thick, dark eyebrows seemed to merge together. "No, I don't believe I do. Surely there's a logical explanation for those voices we heard. A hollow space, maybe, that causes an echo. The voices might be those of guests in an upstairs room, and somehow the sound resonates in the parlor."

"Hadn't thought of that," Polly said, looking at Harriet, who merely shrugged in response. She hadn't thought of that either. Was it even a possibility?

"It's truly bizarre," Matthew declared.

"Speaking of bizarre," Harriet began, hoping to catch the Clutterbucks off guard, "someone at church this morning mentioned seeing you two looking in people's window with your binoculars. You wouldn't happen to be private detectives, would you? I noticed how you tapped the walls in the parlor, as though you've done that sort of thing before."

The two brothers exchanged startled looks while Polly gaped at Harriet in open astonishment.

Suddenly, the twins broke into laughter. Michael said, "Private detectives? What say you, brother? Maybe we should consider changing professions." To Harriet, he added, "Matthew and I are in the plumbing supplies business. Nothing as exciting as detecting."

"And as for looking in people's windows," Michael went on, "it might look that way to someone who doesn't realize we're focusing our binoculars on a particular finch or warbler in a hedge or shrub near the front of a house." He shook his head. "We're going to have to be more careful, Matthew, or we'll be taken up by the constable."

The two brothers shared a chuckle. Polly and Harriet exchanged knowing glances and laughed with them.

Celia was waiting for them at the kitchen door when they returned. "Let's have some tea to settle our nerves," she suggested.

"Brilliant," Polly said approvingly.

"In the parlor," Celia added. "We might hear the noises again."

Harriet couldn't tell if their hostess dreaded the possibility of that happening again, or if she was hoping it would so Harriet and the others could hear the strange sounds for themselves.

They made themselves comfortable in the parlor, and soon Celia returned, followed by a waitress pushing a tea trolley. The scent of warm ginger biscuits came in with them. Harriet noted the lemon poppy seed tea loaf, dainty egg and cress sandwiches, and fresh scones with Devonshire cream and damson plum jam. Even though she was still full after Aunt Jinny's lavish lunch, Harriet couldn't resist the goodies on the tea tray.

Freddie, Will, and Van soon joined them and happily partook of the refreshments.

Celia regarded her husband hopefully.

He shook his head, giving her a rueful smile. "Sorry, sweetheart. Nothing new to report. Don't know what you heard, but it couldn't have come from the cellar."

Then Michael spoke up, explaining his echo theory. Will added his suggestion about bats, mentioning the two he'd discovered in the church belfry. A lively discussion followed. Only Van remained quiet, frowning absently over his cup of tea.

Harriet wasn't sure what he was thinking, but she could guess. She leaned over to him and said in a low voice, "Van, you mustn't think you're responsible. What's going on here at the inn might not have anything at all to do with the car part thefts."

"I know, but I still feel as if I'm letting the Beems down. I was so sure I'd solved this for them, and they believed me. I want to figure out what's going on so I can make that right with them."

Harriet smiled. Van's sense of responsibility for the people in his jurisdiction was part of what made him an excellent officer.

Lowering his voice to a near whisper, he added, "I don't think the twins have anything to do with it, do you?" He tilted his head in their direction.

The two brothers sat on the couch, speaking with Will in animated voices about the possibility of a large bat colony roosting in the church.

"They were here in the parlor with Celia when she heard the voices earlier this afternoon, so they couldn't have made the noises themselves," she reminded him. "At least not this time."

"True." Van gulped his tea. "Maybe I was too hasty in dismissing Nettie Mackenzie as a possible suspect."

"Her niece told me she never leaves her pub, so I don't see how it could be her," Harriet said. There was still the possibility that Nettie was paying someone to do it for her, but Harriet kept that to herself. After all, she was trying to be encouraging.

Van gave her a wry smile. "Why am I not surprised that you've spoken to her niece?"

"Because you know me," Harriet said with a grin. "Anyway, I think we've all been jumping to conclusions much too quickly. Maybe you could do a background check on the brothers to see if they have criminal records. They told us they sell plumbing supplies, and they seem harmless enough. Let's wait on any other theories until the building inspector shares his findings tomorrow. Who knows? It might really be nothing more than an echo from an upstairs bedroom after all."

"Maybe," Van agreed with a lack of enthusiasm that said to Harriet he didn't buy that theory any more than she did.

CHAPTER SIXTEEN

First thing Monday morning, Harriet asked Polly to run some errands with money from their petty cash, including stopping by the pharmacy for a box of long cotton swabs. How had she overlooked those the last time she'd restocked?

Harriet watched Polly's retreating figure and shook her head. It was hard to stay focused these days. Too much on her mind, she supposed. Wedding plans, sick animals, and the strange, unexplained noises at the Quill and Scroll. Not to mention a possible bat roost at the church and the question of how Randy had come across Jane Birtwhistle's dog figurine. What next? The long list of possibilities she'd scribbled on a notepad offered no conclusive insights to the multiple mysteries she was tackling at the moment.

While Polly was gone, Harriet made calls to follow up with several recuperating patients. Then Mrs. Goodwin called to schedule a teeth cleaning for her black Lab. Harriet scheduled the procedure for later in the week and penciled the details in Polly's appointment calendar.

Shortly afterward, Mrs. Braden called with a question about her cat. "Dr. Bailey, my cat Jingles sits in the sun coming through the living room window almost all day, watching birds and the passersby. Can he get sunburned or even skin cancer?"

"Why yes, he can," Harriet answered. Frankly, she was surprised that Mrs. Braden had thought of it. No one else had ever asked Harriet that question before. "His nose, ears, and other areas where the fur is sparse can easily be affected by ultraviolet rays."

The woman sighed heavily. "I was afraid of that. Is there such a thing as sunscreen for cats?"

"Absolutely," Harriet assured her, "but you'll need to make sure the ingredients aren't toxic, because Jingles might ingest them while grooming himself. I can prescribe a safe one, if you'd like."

"Well, I haven't much money," Mrs. Braden confessed. "Is there anything else I could do to protect Jingles?"

"Close your window curtains between ten in the morning until about three in the afternoon," Harriet suggested. "That will protect Jingles from the most harmful rays."

"Oh, I couldn't do that!" Mrs. Braden protested. "Jingles loves looking out the window. That's what he does. I don't want him unhappy and moping. That will put him off his food, and then what?"

Harriet mulled the problem over for a moment. "Perhaps you could get some ultraviolet ray-blocking film? They might sell it in sheets at the hardware store. The film is transparent, so Jingles can enjoy sitting in the window without fear of sunburn."

"That's wonderful," Mrs. Braden said delightedly. "And I daresay the film will help prevent my upholstery from fading in the sun too. Thank you so much, Dr. Bailey. I'm so grateful. Feel free to send me an invoice for your consultation fee."

Harriet chuckled. Mrs. Braden was a widow living on a fixed income. Harriet had no intention of sending her a bill.

She decided to check her case of medicinal samples when she had a moment to spare. Perhaps there was a small tube of sunscreen suitable for Jingles' needs. If so, she'd pass that along. "Happy to help. No charge this time."

"God bless you, Harriet Bailey," the woman said.

"And you, Mrs. Braden," Harriet replied.

She'd barely hung up the office phone when her cell phone gave a familiar ring. She answered with a cheery, "Hi, sweetie. No more bats, I hope."

"None so far," Will said. "But a man named Neville Branson is coming here this afternoon. Says he's a volunteer with the Bat Conservation Trust. You must have told him about my finding the bats in our church belfry. He's coming to check it out for himself. I wonder if you might want to be here to speak with him before he comes to retrieve the bats from your barn. Ronnie Reynolds is coming too."

"Oh, Will, you shouldn't have called a pest exterminator. What will Mr. Branson think, since bats are protected?" Harriet asked. "I'm sure Ronnie wouldn't do anything illegal, but is it a good idea to have him come when the bat trust guy is around?"

"I didn't call Ronnie for the bats. He's just making his usual routine inspection," Will assured her. "I haven't even told him about the bats in the belfry. He's bringing those tall ladders of his, and if he and Neville Branson can locate exactly how the bats are getting into the belfry, that would help. I need to know how bad the problem is and whether it's going to continue. Can you get away?"

"I'll be there if no emergencies arise," she assured him. She prayed there wouldn't be one—either an emergency or a bat roost at the church.

The owner of two cute dachshunds arrived, and Harriet said a hasty goodbye to Will. She took care of the dogs and then administered annual vaccinations for Maryann Bellow's personable goldendoodle. Polly returned in time to help Harriet file the teeth of a black-and-white rabbit under general anesthesia.

Later, after eating a ham sandwich for lunch, Harriet told Polly she was headed to the church.

"More bat problems?" Polly wanted to know.

"Not sure yet. Ronnie Reynolds is coming to do his usual inspection, and a volunteer from the bat trust named Neville Branson will be there too. He'll be picking up the bats afterward. Could you fetch the cage and put it in the utility room? There's no need for Mr. Branson to go traipsing out to the barn. Put on a face mask just to be on the safe side, and don't handle the bats directly."

"You got it. I hope they don't find a colony in the church," Polly said. "I love animals, but I'm not too keen on the thought of sitting in church some Sunday morning and having bats swoop over my head. We'd never have convinced Gran to come to church yesterday if she'd known bats were found in the belfry."

Slinging her purse over her shoulder, Harriet chuckled. "I don't think bats will disrupt our services. They're nocturnal, and they tend to shy away from humans."

On her drive to the church, an idea popped into Harriet's head. She called Van. "I have a quick question."

"Let's have it," he said, sounding like his usual cheerful self. "I hope I have an answer."

Harriet could almost hear the smile in his voice. "Doesn't Donna Coomb live next door to the Beems in that tall, narrow house between the inn and the seawall?"

"Yes, she does. She's Gabriel Mellon's grandmother," Van said, as though reading her thoughts. "I think we had a brief talk about the boy, didn't we? He's been chumming around with the young Danby boy, Randy. Why do you ask?"

"I'm wondering if she's been hearing strange noises in her house too—like the ones Celia insists she's been hearing. After all, the buildings are very close together. Maybe Mrs. Coomb has been bothered by strange noises but hasn't reported them to anyone. It's just a thought."

"And a good one," Van said. "I should have thought of it myself."

"What if the thieves who stashed stolen goods on the Beems' property also stashed stuff on Mrs. Coomb's property as well?" Harriet hoped she didn't sound like a busybody, telling Van how to conduct his official business. Still, she was curious about whether the strange noises were confined to the old inn or not.

"I'll look into it," Van promised. "I never thought to do so, as Mrs. Coomb hasn't filed a complaint. By the way, the Clutterbucks don't have a criminal record. Not even a speeding ticket. They're probably not master criminals in disguise."

Harriet chuckled. "I didn't think so, but thank you for checking."

After saying goodbye, Harriet parked at the church, next to a truck with REYNOLDS PEST REMOVAL emblazoned on the side. A bright blue sedan was parked on the other side. Presumably, it belonged to the volunteer from the bat trust.

The church doors stood wide open. Scrambling out of the van, she said a quick prayer that the building would prove to be bat-free.

As she trotted up the front steps, she met the church secretary coming out, a large red tote bag tucked under one arm.

"Hi, Claire. On your way to lunch?" Harriet asked.

"Yes, I am, and depending on what Ronnie Reynolds and Mr. Branson say about those bats, I may not come back." Her voice quavered. "I know I'm being irrational, because they're a crucial part of the ecosystem and everything, but I don't like bats. I'm not particularly eager to share space with them."

Harriet raised her eyebrows. "Have they found a roost then?"

"They're just beginning the inspection," Claire said. "But I've already told Pastor Will that I can't work here if there's bats in the church. I just can't. Snakes, spiders, and bats. I'm terrified of them. A body can't think straight with such creatures lurking about."

With a twitch of her lips, Harriet replied, "Bats don't lurk, Claire. And they aren't aggressive. They won't attack you. I agree, they're not one of God's most beautiful creatures, but—"

Claire interrupted her with a strangled laugh. "Not by a long shot! Such ugly little faces and those huge, staring eyes. They might even be vampire bats. What then? I've read about vampire bats. They suck the blood right out of your neck."

Harriet couldn't help herself. She laughed out loud. "We don't have vampire bats in England, Claire. Truly, we don't. You don't need to worry about that. And even if we did, vampire bats feed on animals, like cattle and goats."

"I don't care what kind of bats they find. I don't like them." Claire took a deep breath. "I almost didn't come in today for fear the eaves would be full of the nasty little things. Yesterday during the service, I couldn't keep my mind on what the pastor was saying. I kept imagining bats swooping down and getting tangled in my hair." She shuddered. "I couldn't concentrate on the homily or the hymns or anything. And that's a fact. Perhaps it's silly, but I can't help the way I feel."

"Honestly, I don't blame you. I had a similar struggle during the service," Harriet admitted. Normally, she wouldn't have responded at all, but Claire was a friend, and Harriet understood the irrational discomfort around bats.

Claire's face softened. "Thank you for saying that. It makes me feel a little better." Then she hurried to her car, shaking her head and muttering all the way.

Heaving a sigh, Harriet climbed the rest of the steps and entered the church. She meandered through the sanctuary and down the corridor to the various classrooms and offices, following the low murmur of men's voices. She discovered Ronnie, Will, and a third man examining the janitor's closet.

"Hi, Will, Ronnie. You're hard at work, I see." Harriet gave them a smile. "And you must be Neville Branson."

He was tall and pencil-thin, with bright eyes and a winning smile. Harriet liked him right away.

He shook hands with her enthusiastically. "Thank you for calling about the bats. I'll take them off your hands, but I wanted to see the church belfry first. I need to make certain there isn't a roost."

Ronnie touched the brim of his flat tweed cap. "Nice to see you, Doc. I've been telling the pastor and Mr. Branson here that, by law, I can't remove the bats if we find any more up there. I'm just here for my monthly look-about. I want to make that clear." He eyed Neville suspiciously. "Don't want to get in trouble over a protected species. I know the rules, and I follow them."

"And I've assured Neville of the same thing." Will stood with hands on hips, looking slightly forlorn. Harriet's heart went out to him. She was sure he must be feeling helpless in this situation.

"I passed Claire on my way in. She's not a happy camper, as we say back in the States."

"She's threatened to quit," Will informed her glumly.

"You haven't found anything yet?" Harriet asked Ronnie and Neville.

Ronnie shook his head. "Just got here. But if there's a roost inside the church building or up in the belfry, it should be easy to find. Especially when we have two experts who know what to look for. We'll also check the parsonage."

"This is the time of year that bats are most active," Neville added. "But keep your chin up, Pastor. The bats you found might have flown in through an opening in the belfry or even an open door. Their roost may be nearby and not located here at all."

"The front doors are wide open right now," Harriet said.

Will immediately excused himself and hurried away, presumably to shut the doors.

Ronnie ambled down the corridor, examining every square inch of the space and making the occasional note on a clipboard.

Neville followed close behind. "It's not uncommon for young bats to find their way in through any little gap. Baby bats get lost easily enough. Sometimes they fly in where they don't belong and can't find their way out. If they are young bats, they can easily starve or dehydrate. The pastor said the bats he found were small and weak."

"That's correct," Harriet affirmed. "As I told you on the phone, I've kept them safe in a birdcage and have provided them with water." To Ronnie, she said, "Can you plug any holes you find? That would prevent more bats from coming in."

"Yes, as long as I don't find a roost." Ronnie shot Neville a sidelong glance.

Will returned, and Harriet and the other two men followed him to the stairs that led to the belfry. Neville explained how bats send out high-pitched sounds and listen for the echoes to detect an opening out of the room. "The fact that the two bats the pastor found didn't get out the same way they got in suggests that they were young and easily confused. Perhaps there's no roost, just a convenient opening somewhere."

"Are you a veterinarian too, Mr. Branson?" Ronnie asked.

"Not at all. I'm a trained volunteer interested in bats and rescuing those that become grounded, lost, or injured. I had to be fully certified before I was allowed to rescue them, and it's proven to be very rewarding." Neville's enthusiasm was clear in his voice and expression. "Most of the time I answer calls from members of the public and keep written records about those calls. Occasionally, I'm invited to a school or a civic organization to speak about bats. I enjoy that immensely."

Will led the way up to the belfry. While Ronnie and Neville carefully examined every nook and cranny, Harriet surveyed the small room with interest. She'd never been up there before. The space was littered with old crates, coiled ropes, and other items. The walls were lined with wide wooden boards, many warped with age.

Neville pointed to the tall, narrow windows. "The bats must have come through here, but I see no evidence of a roost. I recommend you have Mr. Reynolds cover the openings with a fine mesh netting. That will prevent any more bats from getting in."

Will nodded with relief. "Good to know." To Ronnie, he said, "Can you get these covered while you're here?"

Ronnie nodded. "I've got just the thing. I'll go grab it and my ladder from the lorry."

Harriet took Will's hand and squeezed it.

He beamed at her, his smile easier now that his concern had been addressed. "Thank you for being here for this."

"It's my pleasure," she assured him. She checked her watch. "Unfortunately, I need to go. I have a patient coming in shortly. I need to prepare."

Will arched an eyebrow. "Anything serious?"

"I don't know yet. Someone hit an owl, and they're bringing it in for me to examine."

"Do you need help with that?" Neville asked. "Bats are my specialty, but I can lend a hand with an injured bird in a pinch."

"Thank you for the offer, but there's no need," Harriet said. "My receptionist, Polly Thatcher, is an experienced assistant. Worth her weight in gold. You can follow me back to my clinic if you'd like. The bats are in a birdcage and ready to go."

"I can find the place," Neville said. "We still need to check out the parsonage."

Will escorted them down the stairs and to the front doors, which he had indeed closed and now opened again so Harriet could leave. Ronnie was wrestling with a long extension ladder. Will hurried to lend a hand.

Harriet thanked Neville for his help and returned to her vehicle. She had barely slid behind the wheel when she received a text from Polly reminding her of the upcoming appointment. Harriet texted back that she was on her way and added that Neville Branson would be arriving shortly to pick up the birdcage containing the two ailing bats.

As she drove, Harriet took a moment to thank the Lord that the belfry was not the home to a large family of furry, winged mammals. She knew how relieved Will must be. He had enough on his plate already with sermon preparation, counseling, hospital visits, missions committee meetings, and a wide variety of other tasks—not to mention their wedding coming up in two months. Worrying about bats and how his parishioners felt about sharing the building with them had only added to his stress.

Harriet noticed a girl with dark braids walking her bike along the side of the narrow road. As she grew closer, she realized it was Ava Danby and that the bike had a flat tire. Harriet stopped her vehicle and called out the open window, "Need a lift?"

Ava's face brightened when she recognized Harriet. "Would you mind very much, Dr. Bailey? My bike has a flat."

"I can see that." Harriet hopped out of the Land Rover and opened the back.

Together they lifted the bicycle in and then climbed into the vehicle to resume the short trip down the road. "Your dad can fix it, I suppose," Harriet ventured. "He's a pretty handy fellow, isn't he?"

"Dad can fix just about anything," Ava agreed, a hint of pride in her tone.

Glancing again at her watch, Harriet knew she was pressed for time. Nonetheless, she decided she had to take advantage of this unforeseen circumstance. She hadn't had the opportunity to speak privately with Randy, but perhaps Ava might be able to share something.

"Did you know that Randy gave me the cutest little porcelain dog last week? It's quite valuable, as it turns out. And can you believe it? It actually belongs to Jane Birtwhistle. It's been missing for quite some time. I hope Randy won't mind that I gave it back to her, since it rightfully belongs to her. Where in the world did your brother find it?"

She cut her eyes sideways and noticed Ava's cheeks losing some of their usual rosy color, her shoulders becoming rigid.

"You say it belongs to Miss Birtwhistle? From church?" Ava's voice sounded small and a little frightened.

"Yes, she made a positive identification. There's a mark on the underside that her mother put there many years ago, long before I was born. It's definitely hers."

Ava swallowed hard before muttering, "Oh boy."

CHAPTER SEVENTEEN

"Are you quite positive the dog figurine belongs to Miss Birtwhistle?" Ava asked. Her cheeks were pale beneath her sprinkle of freckles, her eyes wide and anxious.

Harriet could hear a note of fear in the girl's tone. She felt guilty for having put Ava on the spot, but she dismissed the feeling as irrational. If Ava knew that Randy and the Mellon boy were up to some sort of mischief, Harriet needed to get to the bottom of it and soon.

"I'm positive," she said.

"We didn't know," Ava replied in a breathless gush. "I told them—" But she snapped her mouth shut before finishing the sentence. Her lips pressed tightly together in a grim line, she turned to stare out the window.

Harriet urged, "Go on, Ava. What did you tell them? And who are you talking about exactly? Gabriel Mellon and Randy? I don't like to think that Randy may have stolen the figurine. That's not like him. Or you either."

Ava jerked sideways in the front seat to face Harriet. "No, it's not stealing," she insisted with a slight wail. "It's not. Gabriel said so."

Wishing she had time to question Ava more tactfully, Harriet pushed forward. "What else did Gabriel say? If it isn't stealing, what is it? Did Randy find the figurine somewhere?"

Ava was silent for so long that Harriet assumed she was refusing to answer the question.

She was a pretty girl with her long dark hair and bright eyes like her mother's. Thirteen was a difficult age—still a child but on the cusp of young womanhood. Harriet remembered what Doreen had said about her daughter having a crush on Gabriel. No doubt Ava wouldn't want to get him in trouble, but how far would she go to make an impression on the boy?

"What else did Gabriel say?" Harriet asked again.

"He said we shouldn't tell anyone. Not yet at least. Finders keepers and all that." Ava's lower lip trembled.

Curious, Harriet asked, "What did you find, exactly? Besides the porcelain dog."

Ava responded with a vigorous shake of her head. It was obvious she didn't intend to share any more information.

Harriet was convinced that both Ava and Randy wanted to impress Gabriel, the cool city boy. Harriet had no doubt Gabriel was the leader in this little escapade, whatever it was. She fervently hoped the streetwise teen wasn't leading Randy and Ava into trouble—especially of the illegal variety. Tom and Doreen would be furious, not to mention deeply disappointed in their children.

There was no time to pursue the matter. Harriet had reached the lane to the Danby farm. They passed the sheep pen and the large enclosure where the alpacas grazed. Little Terrance, hair tousled as usual, sat on a red tricycle in front of the house. He wore baggy brown shorts and a grubby T-shirt. He also sported what appeared to be a Viking helmet, complete with horns and a nose guard. Such a cute kid. Harriet wondered, not for the first time, if she and Will would be blessed with children one day. She sincerely hoped so.

When she brought the Land Rover to a stop, Ava hopped out immediately, probably hoping Harriet wouldn't ask any more disconcerting questions.

Doreen appeared on the front porch, wearing a floral apron and wiping her hands on an immense dish towel. Even from where she sat, Harriet could see that her friend's apron was dusted with flour. Doreen had been baking again. No surprise. The woman seemed to live in her kitchen.

As Harriet walked around the van to help retrieve Ava's bicycle, Doreen called out to her daughter, "Everything all right, pet?"

"Just a flat tire, Mum," Ava called back.

"Your dad can take care of that quick enough," Doreen assured her.

Ava avoided Harriet's poignant gaze as they wrestled the bike out of the vehicle. Her cheeks were flushed a bright pink. Whether it was from the exertion of lifting the bike, the summer heat, or embarrassment, Harriet couldn't say for sure. "Thank you for the lift," the girl said quietly, not meeting Harriet's gaze.

"You're welcome, Ava, but I wish you'd trust me." She gave her a searching look. "If you need help, I want to give it."

In a near whisper, Ava replied, "Please don't say anything about this to Mum and Dad. Not yet. I need time to think. That's how you can help me."

Harriet raised her eyebrows. What should she do? She didn't want to keep secrets from Doreen and Tom, especially about their children. On the other hand, she wanted to gain Ava's trust.

Finally, she replied in a low voice, "All right. I'll stay quiet for now. But you and Randy need to think about what you're doing and do the right thing. Jane Birtwhistle is eager to have the other figurines returned, if you know where they are. I appreciate Randy's kindness in thinking of me, but the figurine was not his to give away. Perhaps you should tell him what I've told you. And tell Gabriel as well. You'll also need to talk about all of this with your parents. Do you understand?"

Ava gave her a curt nod before pushing her bicycle toward the house.

Doreen waved and took a step or two off the porch. "Harriet, can you stay for a cuppa? I've made fresh scones too. Just took them out of the oven."

Normally, Harriet would have jumped at the chance to indulge in Doreen's famous scones. "I wish I could," she said. "But I've got a patient on the way, an injured owl."

Doreen shook her head. "Poor thing. You'd best be going then. And you may have another patient before the day is through. Our neighbor up the way thinks her goat ate some laundry right off the clothesline. As you know, it's a myth that goats can digest anything, that they have cast-iron stomachs. They really don't. Myrtle's goats can't even eat commercial goat chow."

Harriet waved, hoping she wouldn't have to perform surgery. "Gotta dash, Doreen. Next time I'll take you up on that offer of a scone or two."

Smiling, Doreen said, "You do that, Harriet, and thanks for giving my girl a lift."

Harriet waved as she slid back into the driver's seat. She'd love to stay and chat. She wanted to get to the bottom of what was going on with Randy, Ava, and Gabriel. But she'd have to be patient. She'd promised Ava she wouldn't bring the subject up with her parents—yet. Harriet toyed with the idea of following the kids to find out for herself what they were up to. But when would she find the time?

Neville Branson was loading the birdcage containing the two bats into his vehicle as Harriet parked in her spot at the clinic. "I'll return the cage," he called to her.

"No rush," Harriet called back. "And thanks again for all your help."

"You should come to one of our free seminars," Neville told her. "You can learn all sorts of things about caring for these little guys."

"I just might do that," Harried replied. *Read Jane's mother's World War II journal. Follow Gabriel and the Danby kids. Attend bat seminar. Find source of mysterious noises at the inn.* Her to-do list was growing by the minute.

"This may have been your first encounter with bats up close and personal, as they say, but I doubt it'll be your last. So many caves about, not to mention old buildings full of inviting nooks and crannies. I'm glad we had a happy outcome this time." He waved and climbed into his vehicle.

As usual, Polly had everything ready when Harriet entered the examination room, including two sets of heavy-duty bite-proof gloves for handling the wild owl.

A rather anxious young man with worried eyes presented Harriet with an injured tawny owl in a large cardboard box. It was a beautiful bird, and Harriet sincerely hoped she could restore it to perfect health. She could already tell its wing was broken, but that should be fixable.

Before checking to see if the bird had internal injuries, she examined its head and then the large eyes with their massive pupils. One look through her ophthalmoscope relieved Harriet's fear that the owl might have detached retinas from the collision. If that were the case, the poor creature wouldn't be able to fend for itself again in the wild and would never be able to be released. She breathed a prayer of thanks that the owl's eyes were fine.

"Can you do anything, Doc?" asked the young man, who'd introduced himself simply as Perry. "Will he fly again? I feel ghastly about the whole thing. The bird collided with my windscreen, and I stopped right away to see if it was all right. He's not looking too keen."

Harriet gave him a sympathetic smile. "I can fix the wing, which should be fully mended in a couple of weeks. I'll check for internal injuries too. The eyes are always a major concern with wild birds. Fortunately, his are okay."

Perry nodded. "What will happen to it now?"

"After I repair the wing, if there are no internal injuries, I'll get in touch with some friends of mine in wildlife rehabilitation and see who has room for another rescue. The owl can fully recuperate with them and later be released back into the wild." Since moving to Yorkshire, she'd met several people who worked in wildlife rehabilitation, any of whom would be able to care for the owl while it regained its strength. If neither Martha Banks nor Garth Hamblin had space, and if the bird's only injury was the broken wing, she might even trust Clarence Decker with the task.

Perry breathed out a sigh of relief. "I'm so glad to hear it. I'll be happy to cover its expenses here."

"Oh, I don't charge for things like this," Harriet protested. "I don't think people should be penalized for doing the right thing after an accident. It might discourage them from bringing an injured animal to me in the future."

"Then I'm definitely paying for it," Perry declared. "You shouldn't be penalized for doing the right thing either." He checked the time. "I've got to dash. My lunch break is almost over. Be sure to send me a bill." He rushed out the door, and, with Polly's help, Harriet continued her examination of the injured owl.

The phone rang at reception, and Polly hurried to answer it, removing her gloves as she went. When she returned, she put on the long gloves again and helped set the bird's wing. "I guess I'll give the wildlife rehab center a call," she said.

"Yes, but not right away," Harriet told her. "I want to make sure this handsome fellow recovers a bit before we move him again."

"So it's a male?"

"That's right. What was the phone call about?"

Polly grinned. "Do you have time to x-ray a pygmy goat? That phone call was from Myrtle McKerley. She thinks her goat swallowed a dish towel. Snatched it right off the clothesline."

That would be the neighbor Doreen had mentioned earlier, the woman with the goat that couldn't eat goat chow. "Sure, have her come on in," Harriet said as she carefully transferred the owl to a cage. "And if you could stay to lend a hand in case I need to perform surgery, I'd appreciate it."

"You got it. And speaking of goats, have you ever seen those videos online with baby goats wearing pajamas jumping around in a barn?" Polly asked. When Harriet shook her head, Polly went on enthusiastically. "You've got to watch one. They are so adorable."

Harriet laughed, promising to view the video when she had a moment to spare. Whenever that might be.

The office phone rang again, and Polly dashed off to answer it. Harriet set about tidying the clinic, but her thoughts returned to the mysteries at hand. Had Van had a chance to visit Mrs. Coomb and ask if she'd been hearing strange noises on her property? Had Ronnie been able to cover all the openings in the belfry with the wire mesh? Harriet really hoped so. She shuddered at the idea of bats swooping down on her wedding guests.

The thought of the wedding brought on the dilemma of her bridal gown. She still hadn't found the right one. So many of the ones in bridal magazines were too over the top, fairly bursting with ruffles and frills. Others were too immodest, with long slits up the side of the skirts or too low-cut in the front—hardly the sort of wedding dress that should be worn by a pastor's wife. She'd yet to see many options for the kind of gown that would suit her.

Polly poked her head through the door, interrupting Harriet's musings. "It's Celia Beem for you." She raised her eyebrows and pursed her lips.

Harriet made her way to the front desk to take the call. "Celia, has the building inspector been there?" she asked cheerily.

"He's come and gone," Celia told her. "And, as I suspected, he didn't find anything amiss. The chimney is sound. No bricks are going to fall on our heads. He checked the cellar too, but he thinks perhaps the rattling grate might have something to do with heavy lorry traffic on the road out front."

"No bat roosts either?" Harriet asked.

Celia gasped. "As I live and breathe, I forgot to ask about that."

"Don't worry about it. The inspector would have mentioned it if he'd found one, and I'm sure he would have checked for signs of any animals," Harriet said. "He did make a thorough examination of the building, right?"

"Top to bottom, roof to cellar," Celia assured her.

"Any ideas regarding a possible echo?" Harriet pressed. Physics was not her strong suit, so she had no idea what sort of building construction might lend itself to echoes.

"None. When I suggested that as a possibility, I think he wrote me off as a hysterical female." Celia gave a self-conscious chuckle. "Maybe I am. But I'm so glad the Clutterbuck brothers were with me yesterday when I heard the voices. They heard them too and are still intrigued. At least I know I'm not going mad."

"I'm also glad they were there and they heard what you heard," Harriet agreed. "I only wish I'd heard something. As a vet, I have some practice distinguishing and identifying sounds. My patients can't talk to me, so I've learned to distinguish between regular squeals, grunts, and barks and those that indicate pain or fear. What you call whispering voices, I might describe as something else." She glanced up and noticed Polly listening intently to her side of the conversation.

"Yes, I imagine that's true," Celia replied. "I wish you could have been here when we heard the noises. Maybe next time."

Harriet sincerely hoped there wouldn't be a next time, that the noises would cease altogether. Pursuing an earlier thought, she asked, "Celia, are you acquainted with Mrs. Coomb, who lives next door to you?"

"Not really. Why do you ask?"

"I was wondering whether she's also heard strange noises in her house."

"I suppose I could ask, but what if she thinks I'm crazy? Then again, if she's hearing strange sounds too, that might mean Freddie and I are wrong about someone like Nettie Mackenzie trying to scare us out of business."

"Probably." Harriet stroked her chin. "You know, I've been thinking a bit more about that. If someone is trying to scare you away, they aren't trying very hard, are they?"

"What do you mean?" Harriet could hear the confusion in Celia's voice.

"I mean, why aren't they poisoning your food or releasing rats in the kitchen or something like that? Why aren't they scaring away your guests by making noises in their rooms at night? Not that I want them to, of course, but there are so many worse things that could be happening."

"Stop, Harriet!" Celia sounded alarmed. "For all we know, they're simply starting small. Who knows how they'll escalate?"

CHAPTER EIGHTEEN

Before leaving for the day, Polly asked if she could borrow Harriet's stack of bridal magazines. "I promise I'll bring them back in the morning."

"There's no hurry," Harriet assured her. "I've gone through them all a dozen times. Keep them for as long as you'd like." Then, giving Polly a sidelong glance, she teased, "Is there something you want to tell me?"

Harriet held her breath in anticipation when she observed the sudden blush on Polly's cheeks. Had Van proposed again? Their dating relationship had ended when Van popped the question before Polly was ready, but things were different now, and they were together again. Had Polly accepted this time? Would Harriet's young receptionist be shopping for a wedding gown of her own? She and Van always seemed so happy together, particularly yesterday. They were an adorable couple.

"No," Polly said, her cheeks turning an even deeper shade of pink. "I'm just curious about modern wedding trends and dress styles and stuff. I know you've been busy working out the details for your wedding, and, well, I just want to see what's what, you know? It all seems so complicated—planning a wedding, I mean. There are so many details to think about."

"It is complicated," Harriet admitted with a sigh. "I had no idea. Sometimes when I think about all the decisions I've had to make and all the ones I still need to make, I begin to worry that it'll never get done. Then I take a deep breath and remind myself that everything doesn't have to be decided today, right this very minute. Everything will work itself out in the end—or so Will keeps telling me."

"Have you decided who's gonna perform the ceremony?" Polly asked as she returned a handful of pens to the pencil mug on her desk. "I mean, I assume Will isn't officiating his own wedding."

"I'm leaving that up to Will," Harriet replied. "He has several close friends from his seminary days. I suppose he'll ask one of them to do the honors."

"And what about the wedding cake?" Polly went on. "Barbara at the Happy Cup would be over the moon if you asked her to make it."

Harriet frowned. "How do you know?"

"She told me so when I stopped in last week to pick up those miniature Victoria sponges." Victoria sponge was a well-loved type of cake in the UK, featuring layers of light, fluffy cake with jam, whipped cream, and often fresh fruit. Harriet had come to enjoy the treat immensely. "Barbara's a good baker. She said everyone in the village is talking about you and Pastor Will tying the knot. It's the hot topic around the teacups these days. She says it's all so romantic." Polly grinned.

Harriet felt a blush rising into her cheeks. She wasn't sure how she felt about being the so-called "hot topic around the teacups," as Polly put it.

Polly added, "That's life in a small village. The good news is everybody knows everybody else. The bad news is everybody knows everybody else's business."

"Yes, I've become aware of that this past year," Harriet said. Although she didn't say it aloud, she did find it rather amusing that everyone was talking about her and Will's upcoming nuptials. But on the other hand, it was also embarrassing. Surely Polly was exaggerating.

But if Harriet knew one thing about Polly, it was that she could trust her. In fact, Polly had been true-blue since Harriet arrived in Yorkshire a year ago, smoothing her way with the locals, helping her find her feet with the vet clinic, and educating her on local customs and vocabulary. Harriet had been blessed with some good friends in the States, but she'd never felt closer to anyone than Polly.

While her upcoming wedding was on her mind, Harriet wondered if this would be an appropriate time to ask Polly if she'd be willing to serve as her maid of honor.

But before she could do so, Polly asked, "Any word yet from Pastor Will about keeping bats out of the belfry?" She powered off her computer and tidied her desk.

"Nothing yet, but he texted me there'd been an emergency with one of his parishioners and he had to go to the hospital in Whitby to support the family. He promised to call when he could." Harriet was getting used to such incidents after rescheduling countless dates, either because there was an emergency with a member of Will's flock or one of her own patients. They had certainly begun to master flexibility in their scheduling with each other.

After retrieving the bridal magazines, Polly slung her shoulder bag over one arm, saying, "That's the life of a minister for you. Always on duty—kind of like a veterinarian." She winked at Harriet.

"You just never know when you're going to be interrupted. I'll see you in the morning." She started toward the door.

Perhaps it wasn't the ideal moment, but given how short the engagement was, Harriet couldn't afford to waste time. "Polly, wait." When Polly turned with a questioning smile, she continued, "You've been the best friend anyone could ever ask for. I was wondering if you'd be willing to be my maid of honor."

Polly's jaw dropped, and her eyes grew wide. "Really? You mean it?"

Harriet laughed at the comically shocked expression on her friend's face. "Of course I mean it, silly. What do you think?"

Polly squealed, dropped the pile of magazines on an end table, and dashed across the room to fling her arms around Harriet. "I'd love to be your maid of honor! Thank you, Harriet. I'm so honored. I can hardly wait to tell Mum and Dad. Van too." She pulled back and peered into Harriet's face. "You know you're my best friend too, right?"

"I hope so," Harriet teased. She'd known Polly would agree, but it was lovely to have the confirmation. "Thanks, Polly. I'm so glad you'll be standing up with me."

Polly beamed at her. "I wouldn't miss it for the world. How can I support you? What do you need? What kind of dress should I wear—short, long, sleek, or frilly? Any ideas for colors yet? Should I wear a hat?"

"I'm still mulling all that over. It's a bit overwhelming," Harriet said. Then, pointing to the bridal magazines, she added, "If you see anything in there that tickles your fancy, let me know. I'm flexible. Maybe we can both find a wonderful dress to wear. Nothing too fancy, though."

"That's okay by me. I'm into simpler styles myself." Polly smacked herself on the forehead. "I can't believe I almost forgot to tell you. I heard from Van. He visited Mrs. Coomb and asked if she'd been hearing strange noises."

"He did?" Harried asked eagerly. "Has she heard anything?"

Polly grimaced. "Sorry to disappoint, but not a thing. And she seemed rather surprised he would ask."

Harriet sighed. "Thanks for the update. I hope he didn't tell her about Celia Beem's strange noises. Mrs. Coomb might think she has a pair of kooks for neighbors."

"Van has more discretion than that," Polly assured her. "He explained about the arrest of the car-part thieves and told her he was simply making follow-up inquiries. That's all. Mrs. Coomb had read about the arrest in the paper, so she seemed satisfied with his explanation."

"You're right. I know Van well enough to know that about him by now. Did he learn anything else?"

Polly tilted her head to one side and pursed her lips. "Actually, he did. Mrs. Coomb is away from the house all day. She works at the bank. If Celia is hearing those voices during the day, Mrs. Coomb wouldn't know if they could be heard in her house or not. Her grate could be jumping and all sorts of whispery sounds could be coming from her cellar, but she wouldn't know anything about it unless she happened to hear something on her days off."

"I hadn't thought of that." Suddenly Harriet wondered if she should ask Van to speak with Gabriel Mellon. The boy was staying in Mrs. Coomb's house for the summer. Perhaps he'd heard the strange noises and never thought to mention them to his grandmother. If he was made of sterner stuff than Celia Beem, he might not be bothered by odd sounds. He might assume anything he heard was related to old pipes and gurgling drains or traffic passing by.

On the other hand, if she asked Van to continue pursuing the situation by questioning Gabriel, would Van think she was interfering with his job? Dictating his investigation? Sticking her nose where it didn't belong? Harriet decided to keep the idea to herself for now. Maybe Van was way ahead of her on this. He was a professional, after all. He didn't need an amateur sleuth telling him what to do.

Perhaps she should speak with Gabriel herself. It would give her an opportunity to get to know him a little better. She wanted to take him out to meet Clarence Decker and show him the teen's menagerie of animals. She suspected Gabriel would enjoy that. He seemed to have a real interest in animals. Maybe he wasn't as tough as he pretended to be.

But she could figure that out later. She hugged Polly again. "Thanks for agreeing to be my maid of honor. And for the update from Van. I appreciate his indulging my amateur attempts at detecting. He's a good man."

Polly blushed. "He is."

"I can't help wondering what your grandmother thinks of him," Harriet mused.

Polly laughed. "Don't ask. Gran doesn't like most people outside our immediate family circle. And even we aren't exempt from her criticism. I try to pay her no mind and remain polite and respectful."

"Seems like the wise thing to do," Harriet agreed. "See you in the morning."

Polly waved, retrieved the bridal magazines, and left with a bounce in her step.

An hour or so later, Harriet heard a firm knock at the front door of her house. Hoping it was Will, she dashed to open it. The person on the doorstep was every bit as welcome.

"I brought you some of the blueberry buckle you didn't get to eat yesterday," Aunt Jinny said, holding out a dish covered with tinfoil. "And to be perfectly honest, I can't stand the suspense any longer. What on earth happened at the Quill and Scroll? Did you catch a thief? Snag a spook? Tame the bucking grate?"

Harriet laughed as she ushered her aunt into the house. "I'm sorry. I should have called, but with one thing and another, I completely forgot." She led the way to the kitchen and put the kettle on for tea to go with the blueberry buckle. Harriet hadn't had dinner yet, but she wasn't very hungry. A refreshing cup of tea and a slab of her aunt's blueberry-studded dessert would be just the thing.

"Start at the beginning," Aunt Jinny said, settling in a chair at the table. "Don't leave anything out."

Over dessert and tea, Harriet summarized what had taken place the day before in the guest parlor at the Quill and Scroll.

Aunt Jinny seemed particularly intrigued that the Clutterbuck brothers had heard the voices as well. "But you didn't hear anything, right?"

"I heard nothing—not even a peep," Harriet said. "I wish I had. I'm sure Celia was hoping we would hear something while we were there. She'd be doubting her own sanity by now if it weren't for Michael and Matthew Clutterbuck. Like I said, they were in the parlor at the time and heard the whispering for themselves. So now we know for certain she's not imagining things."

"Unless the Clutterbucks are going along for the fun of it," Aunt Jinny suggested, dropping a sugar cube into her second cup of tea.

"No, I don't think so. They seemed concerned and curious, and I don't think they were pretending. Besides, Van checked into their backgrounds. No criminal record. They're clean, ordinary businessmen, like they claim to be. Regardless of what Callista Thatcher thinks." Harriet explained Polly's grandmother's suspicions about the brothers, getting a good chuckle from her aunt.

Aunt Jinny sipped her tea and seemed lost in thought for a moment. "You know, perhaps more than one thing is going on over there at the same time. A rattling grate could be caused by one thing, and faint whispering voices caused by something else. How do we know the two incidents are related?"

"Good point, but even if they're unrelated, I have no idea what's causing either one. Celia called earlier today and told me about the building inspector's report. According to him, everything is perfectly fine. Their chimney isn't losing a brick here and there. The foundation is secure." Harriet took another bite of the blueberry buckle. She particularly liked the tart lemon glaze on top.

"What did Van have to say about it all?" her aunt asked.

"He's as puzzled as I am. When we were at Celia's, he said that maybe he'd been in too much of a hurry to dismiss Nettie Mackenzie as a suspect. Maybe she really is making a feeble effort to sabotage their business."

"I doubt it," Aunt Jinny replied. "Nettie might spread rumors, but she'd hardly make noises that only the Beems can hear. Successful sabotage would involve scaring away customers. And rather than making quiet whispery noises in the parlor, she should be jolting the upstairs guests out of a sound sleep with horrendous screeching and other noises everyone can hear."

"That's what I told her," Harriet said. "Do you know Nettie?"

"Not very well. She's not one of my patients, and I've never eaten at her place. She's a tough one though. If she made up her mind to run the Beems out of business, she'd do more than spread rumors. That being said, I doubt she'd risk trespassing. As a business owner, Nettie can't afford to end up in court."

"No matter how many theories I go through, I can't land on a single one with enough evidence to support it." Harriet finished her food and pushed away her empty plate, deciding to change the subject to a less frustrating one. "Did I mention that a volunteer from the Bat Conservation Trust came to the church today to check for a roost in the belfry? Ronnie Reynolds was there too, doing his regular pest inspection."

"And what happened?"

"Much to Will's relief and mine, they didn't find a bat roost. But they did find several possible points of entry." Harriet told her aunt what Neville said about bats and how to prevent them from getting in. "It must have taken Ronnie all afternoon to put up the wire mesh that Neville recommended. From what I've read about them, bats in the UK are small, so they can easily squeeze into gaps in the stonework and through cracks under and over doors. I might look into taking some classes and getting certified to care for bats in the future. I didn't like feeling helpless when those two were in my care. I couldn't do much for them."

"Let's hope the coast is clear," Aunt Jinny said. "At least the belfry is okay. I did a little online research the other night too. I don't know much about bats, but I was concerned about what illnesses might be spread through them."

"You're not the only one who's concerned," Harriet said. "On my way into the church, Claire was coming out. She was horrified by the idea of sharing the building with a family of bats. She told Will she might quit if they found a colony."

Aunt Jinny sighed. "I'm sure Will is greatly relieved. I know I am. I suppose he'll make an announcement at church this Sunday. At least I hope he will. It will ease everyone's mind to know that our belfry is bat-free and now hopefully bat-proof."

After her aunt said good night and returned to her own cottage, Harriet took a shower and released Maxwell from his harness. She picked up her cell and checked to see if she'd missed any calls or texts from Will. She hadn't.

As she crawled into bed, she prayed that all was well at the hospital. She prayed too that she could put aside her various worries and get some sleep. *Let go and let God.*

CHAPTER NINETEEN

White Church Bay
July 1941

Flory dipped a toothpick into the bottle of red nail polish and placed a tiny dot on the bottom of the Staffordshire figurine. She'd mentally wrestled with how best to divide them up, putting half in the crate she'd begged from the greengrocer and the other half in the sea chest Dad provided—a chest that had once belonged to a long-ago seafaring uncle. Or had the uncle been a fisherman? Dad couldn't recall. He'd traded a basket of fresh cabbages and leeks for a bale of straw. Flory was using this to pad the crate and chest, hoping it would be sufficient to keep the figurines safe.

Earlier in the week, Dad had accompanied Miss Dingle and several others to investigate the smugglers' tunnel located near the inn. Dad declared it stable and decided it was a suitable place to store a number of boxes, crates, and chests safely. He hadn't told her where the entrance to the cave was located, and Flory was fine not knowing.

"So it's really all right then?" she had asked. "We can hide these things away safely?" She was planning for the crate to go to the tunnel.

He'd given her a curt nod in response. "You can pack up your little treasures," he said. "Though it seems like a foolish idea, if you ask me. How do we know someone won't tell the Germans where we've hidden the stuff? They might torture some poor soul to get the information out of them. Might be best, when all is said and done, to bury these things in the garden."

Flory didn't know what to say to that. Nor did she press her father to find out exactly where in the garden he would bury their belongings. For a moment, she wondered if perhaps she should ask about the tunnel's location.

But she had too much on her mind already, and there were others who knew where the tunnel was. The sea chest would be hidden at the church somewhere. She wondered if she should tuck a letter inside, something that might be of use to identify her as the owner. She contemplated placing her journal in the sea chest, but she'd only just started keeping a daily record of her activities. The letter would have to be enough.

Flory reached for another figurine. Her father sat at the other end of the kitchen table, sharpening a knife. He'd been quietly pensive since he came home for his noon meal. She supposed he had a lot on his mind too.

A large bowl of cherries filled the kitchen sink. The fruit needed to be pitted and turned into preserves. Flory should have done it first thing in the morning, while it was still cool outside, but Jane had been particularly fussy because of the heat. Flory had been distracted, trying to soothe her.

She had finally gotten the baby down for a morning nap, but she still couldn't concentrate on the cherries. She was eager to get the figurines packed away as soon as possible.

The day before, Flory had examined the various family papers locked away in the small desk in her parents' room: Dad's discharge papers from the army after the first war, her marriage license, Jane's birth certificate, the deed to the cottage, her mother's obituary from the newspaper.

Flory had considered wrapping these in a bit of waterproof oilskin and tucking them inside the old sea chest. "What do you think, Dad?"

"Better not," he replied. He sounded as unsure as she felt. "We might need them in a hurry."

She retrieved two more figurines from the mantel and carried them back to the kitchen. She was in the middle of dabbing a red dot on the bottom of the first one when Marietta Trumble stopped by, fresh in a dotted Swiss garment despite the summer heat. Flory, hot and irritable, felt a pang of envy.

"Hi there, Flory. My, it's hot today, isn't it? We could use a bit of rain. My roses are drooping. I thought I'd come by for a bit of a chin-wag," Marietta babbled cheerfully. "Hello, Mr. Woodley."

Dad acknowledged her with a slow, mumbled greeting.

"Packing up your treasures, I see. Mine are done. Don't guess they're valuable to anyone but Simon and me, but they're safe now. These figurines are quite whimsical, aren't they?" Marietta picked up a porcelain giraffe and then set it down again. "Why are these on their sides?" She made a sweeping gesture across the table.

"They're drying. I'm putting a dot of nail polish on the bottom of each one," Flory explained. "That way, if they get mixed up with someone else's belongings, I'll know which figurines are mine. It seems everyone has Staffordshire porcelain of some kind. Mum told me once how popular it is."

"Good idea." Marietta pulled out a chair and sat down at the table. "Are these going in the chest too?" She indicated a silver spoon and an amethyst brooch sitting on the table.

Flory nodded. The spoon had been a gift from Jane's godmother on the baby's christening day. The brooch had belonged to Flory's mother, a wedding present. The objects weren't very valuable, unlike the porcelain figurines, but Flory didn't want the Nazis to get their hands on them.

"I wonder what will happen to all of this if we don't survive the war?" Flory mused aloud.

Both her father and her friend dismissed the idea with startled exclamations.

Flory gave a rueful laugh. "I know. It's not to be thought of. But suppose that's what happens? And what if someone many years from now discovers these figurines? Maybe folks will laugh, thinking how foolish I was for hiding them away."

"I imagine they'll think they found a pirate's treasure trove," Marietta joked. "At least the stuff they find in the smugglers' tunnel."

Flory shrugged. "Perhaps. Figurines aren't useful or anything. They might wonder why we bothered to hide such things at all."

"Not useful yet," Marietta quipped. "Who knows? Someone in the War Office in London could come up with a way to make them useful for the war effort before all is said and done. They'll put out a bulletin calling for all patriotic citizens to donate their Staffordshire china to turn into bomb parts or something." She chuckled. "Yesterday, I pulled all the metal coat hangers from our closet."

"Why?" Flory asked, startled. "What are you doing with those?" She dotted the last figurine and replaced the lid on the nail polish bottle.

"The Ministry of Aircraft Production needs more metal. There was an article in yesterday's paper and an announcement over the wireless, urging us to part with our coat hangers and shoe trees and anything made of aluminum. They'll even take any old saucepans we can spare."

"Must be for aeroplane parts." Dad rose and made his way to the kitchen sink.

"That's it exactly," Marietta said. "Can you imagine turning our little household items into parts for Spitfires and Hurricanes?"

Flory reached over to give Marietta's hand a squeeze. "You're a loyal citizen, Marietta, and a kind neighbor. You and Simon both. You set a good example for the rest of us."

Marietta blushed. "We surely try. 'Do unto others,' as the Good Book says."

"Dad, will you have a cup of tea?" Flory asked.

Dad, who was now standing by the back door of the kitchen, slapped on his cap. "I'm going out. I'll return for my supper." He left after bidding Marietta a good day.

"Did you hear that Mr. Hocking died the other day?" Marietta asked, accepting a cup of tea.

Flory collapsed into the nearest chair, weak-kneed at the news. "Mr. Hocking? What happened?"

"He just dropped dead." Marietta added a pinch of sugar to her cup before taking a sip. "His wife said he was never sick a day in his life and it must have been stress. They're saying it was a heart attack."

"Oh, I'm so sorry to hear it." Flory took a gulp of tea from her cup, scalding her tongue in the process. The pain took her mind off the shock of the sad news and her worried thoughts about Donald. She'd liked Mr. Hocking. She remembered his recent kindness in giving her the humbug.

"I was just in his shop last month, buying a journal," Flory went on. "Miss Dingle suggested I keep a daily record about what's happening here on the home front so Donald can read all about it when he returns. Or Jane might be interested when she's older."

Her eyes watered, but she couldn't weep. Flory had cried plenty at the beginning of the war and even more since she'd hugged Donald goodbye at the station in Scarborough. But she'd been unable to cry for the last few days. In fact, Flory was beginning to suspect that she had no tears left.

CHAPTER TWENTY

Will finally called around half past eleven. "I'm sorry to call so late, but I knew you'd be worried if you didn't hear from me."

"You were right. I'm glad you called," Harriet assured him groggily. Rubbing the sleep from her eyes, she added, "I don't care how late it is. I'm always glad to hear from you no matter what. It's good to hear your voice." She stretched and rubbed the top of Charlie's head. The cat yawned and moved to the foot of the bed. *Sorry to have disturbed you,* Harriet thought with a smile.

"I feel the same way about you," Will said.

"So can you tell me what happened?" Harriet asked.

"You know Mr. Snart, our organist?"

"Yes," Harriet said. "Goodness, is he all right?"

"He's fine, though worried. His forty-year-old son lives over in Whitby and had a heart attack earlier today. Poor Mr. Snart went all to pieces, so I offered to drive him to the hospital and stayed with him until the doctors reported that his son was stable. He was in no condition to drive like that."

"Of course you did," Harriet said fondly. It was so like Will to take things in hand and lend his calm and guidance as a haven in a terrifying situation. "I'm proud of you."

"I'm only doing what I'm called to do," Will said. Harriet could hear him yawning. "Sorry about that, but I just walked through the door. I'll call you later in the morning, love. Right now, I need to get some sleep. I'm so tired I can barely keep my eyes open."

"Love you," Harriet said. "Sweet dreams." She snuggled back under the covers with Charlie nestled at her feet. All was right with the world.

On Tuesday morning Harriet woke in high spirits, ready to face the day. She was determined to find some answers to the many questions that had hounded her thoughts for the past several days.

She retrieved her notepad and reviewed her scribbled notes. For starters, she needed to know exactly where Randy Danby had gotten the porcelain figurine of the King Charles spaniel. She intended to pin him down and get a straight answer out of him once and for all. No excuses.

She grabbed her phone and texted Will to get another question answered. BAT ROOST IN THE PARSONAGE?

Will answered, NO. BUT MADE AN INTERESTING DISCOVERY.

Intrigued, Harriet knew she'd have to wait until later for more details, but for now, knowing Ronnie hadn't discovered bats inside the rest of the church building or the parsonage was a huge relief.

Her morning did not go exactly as she'd planned. Instead of having the opportunity to track Randy down for that heart-to-heart conversation with him, Harriet had her hands full with both scheduled and unscheduled visits with furry and feathered patients, plus checking on the owl between appointments. She was heartened to see that he was taking a little food and water, and Polly had several inquiries out to their wildlife rehabilitation contacts, waiting to see who could take him in. Harriet's friends wouldn't leave her high and dry. If none of them could help the owl, they would provide recommendations for someone who could.

She'd just finished treating a sweet lop-eared rabbit for an ear infection when Doreen arrived at the clinic with a plate of scones. From the fragrance that wafted in with her, Harriet guessed they must be warm from the oven. "I come bringing good cheer and sustenance," she announced, still wearing an apron over her Henley shirt and jeans.

"Apricot almond?" Harriet asked hopefully. Doreen never made a bad scone, but apricot almond was Harriet's favorite.

Doreen confirmed this with a smile. "I even added toasted oats on top."

Polly hopped up from behind her desk. "This calls for a fresh pot of tea."

"Let me wash my hands, and I'll have one right now," Harriet said. The hectic morning had left her hungrier than she'd realized. "I'm so grateful for you. You must have heard my stomach rumbling."

"I did, actually. Having a brood of youngsters means I can hear hunger a mile away." With a chuckle, Doreen placed the plate of scones on the corner of Polly's desk and followed Harriet into an exam room. As Harriet washed her hands, Doreen said quietly, "I actually came to have a word with you in private, if that's all right."

"Of course," Harriet replied as she dried her hands. "Do you want to sit?" She indicated a chair near the examination table.

Doreen closed the door quietly before dropping into the designated chair. "Nothing against Polly, but I need this to stay between you and me for now. You'll be thinking I'm a terrible friend and poor neighbor for letting you down after I'd promised to speak with Randy and still haven't given you an update on what I learned."

"I figured either you were busy or that what he told you was between you and him," Harriet said.

"I did have a chance to speak with him, but I didn't learn much. He said he found the little dog in an abandoned crate filled with rubbish and other discarded things. He said he didn't realize it was valuable, and I'm sure that's true enough. I didn't have time to press him about exactly where he found the crate, because Tom came in looking for him. Needed an extra hand for a minor equipment repair."

Harriet touched her friend's shoulder. "It's okay, Doreen. I understand. I told you I intended to have a talk with Randy myself, and I haven't gotten around to it either. I need to find out exactly where he found that crate. For all we know, it contained more items that Randy doesn't realize might be worth something. If he tossed it away, I want to try to retrieve it. I'd hoped to wrap up this matter today, but now I'm not sure I'll get it done."

Doreen replied with a roll of her eyes. "Life happens. Besides, Tom took Randy with him to Whitby today. We're upgrading our shearing equipment. He wanted me to go with them as well, but little Terrance has strep throat, and some mystery predator has been raiding my henhouse. I suggested he take the Mellon boy along instead. Tom wasn't eager to do so, but I think he will. I feel sorry for that kid. Tom does too."

"Poor Terrance. He seemed fine at church."

"It came on quite suddenly. The little chap is feeling absolutely miserable. Even eating ice cream for breakfast isn't cheering him up. Ava's with him now, but she has other chores to do today, so I can't be away too long."

Harriet's thoughts shot back to the brief conversation she'd had with Ava when she'd given the girl a lift the previous afternoon. Randy, Ava, and Gabriel were up to something—of that she was certain. Ava's manner had been worried, evasive. Randy might indeed have found the dog figurine in an old crate filled with what he presumed to be junk, as he'd told his mother, but where had he found the crate? And why was he being so cagey? Was it possible he knew where Jane's missing figurines could be found?

"Honestly, I'm still trying to catch up from lambing season," Doreen went on. "But sooner or later, one of us will manage to have a sit-down with Randy, and then we'll get the whole scoop." Doreen spread her hands over her knees. "Most days I don't know whether I'm coming or going. This time of year is always busy."

"I understand that completely," Harriet assured her. "Some days I'm so distracted, I can hardly focus on my patients. I've been that way since Will brought me those two bats." She didn't mention she'd also been distracted by Jane's claim to the dog figurine and her concerns that the Danby kids might be keeping a secret, not to mention how someone or something was making disturbing noises at the old Quill and Scroll Inn.

"Bats in the belfry. We heard about those through the grapevine." Doreen shook her head. "Hope there's not a roost up there in the belfry, the rafters, or anywhere else. I reckon people might quit coming to services if that's the case."

"There are no bats making their home in the church," Harriet announced happily. "A volunteer with the Bat Conservation Trust went up there and reassured us there's no roost. He cleared the parsonage as well. He was also able to give Ronnie Reynolds instructions on how to help keep any more bats from winding up in there. Last I knew, Ronnie was sealing possible entrances with a fine wire mesh."

"If there's no roost in the belfry, what were the bats doing up there?" Doreen asked.

"The bats Will found were young and must have strayed from home. They flew into the belfry and became too weak and confused to fly out again. At least, that's what the bat trust volunteer thought. So that's good news. I'm going to speak with Will and get a more detailed update, but as it stands now, we can assume that after a thorough examination, the church building and the parsonage are certified bat-free."

Doreen chuckled. "That's good news indeed. But the pastor is going to have to learn to keep the front doors closed. I know he likes to open them now and again to let the fresh air circulate, but he's tempting the bats to come in that way."

"I think he mainly does that during the day, when bats wouldn't be active, but I'll remind him to close them again before dusk." Harriet sniffed and caught the tantalizing aroma of fresh tea. "Let's go have tea. I hear your scones calling my name."

Rising, Doreen said, "I appreciate the offer, but I need to get on. Thank you for understanding, Harriet. I'll talk with Randy again. You can count on it. I just don't know when. There's no rush, is there?"

"I suppose not," Harriet replied hesitantly. Or was there? On one hand, the figurines had been missing for decades, but on the other hand, Jane Birtwhistle wasn't getting any younger. If her belongings were scattered over the countryside, sitting in bins at rummage sales or the like, shouldn't something be done soon? And if Randy had found the entire crate the figurines had been packed in, shouldn't he return it to Jane at once? "On second thought, I'd like to get to the bottom of things sooner rather than later. Maybe I can drop by this evening and have a word with Randy, and Ava too."

"Anytime," Doreen said.

She followed Doreen out into the main office, where Polly was already enjoying a cup of tea and a scone.

"These are so good," Polly told Doreen between bites.

Harriet helped herself to a scone and promptly pinched off a bite. "I can hardly wait for my mother to try one of these the next time she visits. She'll insist that you share your recipe."

"Happy to do it," Doreen replied, blushing with pleasure.

"Did Harriet tell you I'm going to be her maid of honor?" Polly asked.

Doreen glanced from Polly to Harriet and grinned from ear to ear. "I'm pleased to hear it. I've been wondering who might be asked to stand up with you and Will. Have you decided on a cake? And what about flowers? Have you gone shopping for a dress?"

Harriet chuckled. "I haven't decided on anything except the groom and the maid of honor."

"Those are arguably two of the most important choices, so you're prioritizing well," Doreen told her.

"There are so many decisions to make, even for a simple wedding. I've started a list. I don't really care who ties the knot for us, as long as the knot is good and tight. 'Till death do us part' and all that."

"Right you are," Doreen said. She hugged both of them and took her leave.

And while Harriet always enjoyed seeing her friend, she wished Doreen had left her with more answers than questions.

Will arrived around one o'clock with a white cardboard box, rather like a bakery box.

Harriet eyed it dubiously. "Please don't tell me you've found another bat."

Polly gave a resigned sigh and picked up the phone, likely preparing to call the bat trust again.

He gave them a rueful smile. "No, it's a steak and kidney pie. Still warm too. Mrs. Trumble brought it by to thank me for sitting with her husband last week. I thought we could have lunch on the patio together."

Harriet brightened. "What a lovely idea. Want to join us, Polly?"

Polly dismissed the idea with a languid hand. "No, you lovebirds enjoy yourselves. I brought a sandwich. I thought I'd take Maxwell for a short trot along the bluffs and have my lunch up there. It's such a beautiful day."

Harriet agreed. It was a perfect summer day for an alfresco meal. She removed her white coat and bustled about the kitchen, loading a tray with plates and forks and other items needed to enjoy Mrs. Trumble's savory pie.

Will filled a glass with water and another with iced tea for Harriet at her request. "Why would anyone want to drink cold tea with ice?" he teased her as they made their way out to the table. "It's beyond my understanding. You Americans have never properly respected tea."

Harriet chuckled. "I know. It's disgraceful, really. Good thing the UK has never lowered itself to ice its tea." She knew full well that iced tea had become more popular there in recent decades.

She wasn't all that hungry after Doreen's scone, but she was always eager to spend time with Will. And as Polly had rightly pointed out, it was a gorgeous day. The scent of roses perfumed the air. A profusion of delphiniums, snapdragons, foxglove, and dahlias surrounded the patio. Bees buzzed among the lavender. How blessed she was to have inherited such an idyllic home.

"So, tell me everything that happened with the bat situation after I left yesterday." She sliced the pie and then served Will a hefty portion and herself a smaller one. After all, at the pace she'd been going today, she should probably have something more substantial in her stomach than a scone.

Will gave her a brief rundown of the precautionary measures Ronnie had taken so no more stray bats would fly into the belfry or squeeze through various chinks and cracks in the old building. "Hopefully the church will remain bat-free for a long time to come. That means Claire will not desert me. I still have a secretary."

"That's wonderful news, Will," Harriet said. "I'm so glad. You must be relieved."

"And grateful too," Will replied. "I've been sending up prayers of thanksgiving ever since Ronnie and Neville assured me that all's well." He savored a bite of the pie before asking, "Any wedding updates I should be aware of?"

"Polly agreed to be my maid of honor," Harriet said, beaming.

"Excellent. I can't think of a more perfect choice. Oh, and my roommate from seminary, Jared, has agreed to perform the ceremony."

"That's great. Thank you for taking care of that." Then Harriet remembered Will's earlier text. "By the way, you mentioned something about making a discovery. If it wasn't a bat roost, what did you find?"

Will leaned forward, his eyes gleaming with excitement. "You won't believe it. Ronnie wanted to explore the crypts, just out of curiosity. And guess what we found hidden away down there? Two old crates, and a seaman's chest that belonged to a Florence Birtwhistle. I'm assuming that's Jane's mother, right?"

Harriet's heart skipped a beat. "It is! Did you open the chest or either of the crates?"

"Of course. The chest wasn't locked, and there was a letter inside signed by Florence. It explained about the figurines and why she'd hidden them away—to keep them safe in case of a Nazi invasion. The crates were nailed shut but labeled on the outside with names. One was Trumble. I didn't recognize the name on the other box. Anyway, we didn't open those, because we didn't have the tools with us. Ronnie helped me carry them to my office before he left."

"And you saw the figurines inside the seaman's chest?" Harriet pressed. "Jane will be thrilled."

"We didn't take them out," Will explained. "I moved a bit of packing material around just to see what was inside. Definitely figurines. There's one of a woman riding a horse. I thought it might represent Lady Godiva at first, but the woman is wearing a flowing gown. There was a silver spoon too, wrapped in an old newspaper dated July 1941. Hard to believe the stuff has been down there all this time."

"Amazing, isn't it?" Harriet agreed. "But as Doreen was telling me earlier today, life happens. People get busy with one thing and another, and before you know it, details fall through the cracks. Besides that, Jane told me that her mother had to care for her father—Jane's grandfather—when he became ill. Then he died before he could tell Florence where the chest was hidden."

"Well, I'll make sure Jane's belongings are returned to her as soon as possible," Will said. "I'll call Van too. He can help me return the boxes to their rightful owners."

"This is so exciting," Harriet said. "Makes me wonder if we should do some more exploring to see what else we can find." She took Will's hand. "Would you mind letting me call Jane to tell her the good news? I would really love to do that."

"It's only right for you to be the one to let her know, since you've been involved with this from the beginning. And I don't mind doing more exploring as long as we don't find any more bats," Will said with a laugh. "Who knows? There might be little treasures hidden behind those old, warped wall panels up in the belfry."

Harriet was just about to tell Will about the crate that Jane's grandfather had hidden when their conversation was interrupted. Polly ran up, with Maxwell scampering at her heels. "Harriet, I'm so sorry, but the Trueloves just called. Their cow is having a difficult labor, and they need you."

Harriet stood and kissed Will's temple. "Duty calls."

"No worries. I'll take care of the dishes," he assured her.

"And I'll take care of everything else," Polly said. "I'll reschedule your afternoon appointments. Bringing a baby cow into the world takes a while."

"I'll call you later," Harriet told Will, who was already clearing the table.

"Good," he replied. "I'll want to hear all about the calf."

Harriet dashed off to change into overalls and her wellies. She fetched her medical bag, double-checking to make sure she had everything she needed for a difficult birth. She stowed everything in the back of the Land Rover then jumped into the driver's seat and took off.

It was well after dark when Harriet returned home, dirty and exhausted. It had been a stressful and challenging afternoon. But she'd helped bring a beautiful little heifer safely into the world, and she glowed with satisfaction. She would never tire of the delight that came with helping an animal in need.

The grateful Trueloves had treated her to a feast afterward and served her gooseberry pie for dessert. Experiencing the perfect blend of tart and sweet, Harriet toyed with the idea of planting gooseberries in her own garden.

After showering and catching up on her messages from Polly, Harriet called Will to wish him a good night.

"There you are," he said warmly. "How are you?"

"I'm weary to the bone, but happy," she said.

"That means everything went okay, right?" he asked.

"Yes, the calf is healthy, and the mother is fine. It's days like this that remind me I'm exactly where I'm meant to be." She told him about the late supper the Trueloves had fed her, making a particular point of praising the gooseberry pie.

"You're making me drool," Will said with a chuckle.

"They treated me like a celebrity," Harriet said. "Who knew something as silly sounding as gooseberry pie could taste so delicious?"

"Everyone born and raised in the UK," he teased.

First thing Wednesday morning, Harriet checked on the owl, pleased to see that he seemed to be recovering nicely.

While she brewed a pot of coffee, she checked her emails and found one from Neville Branson, thanking her again for her part in helping to rescue the bats and assuring her that he would be returning her birdcage in the next week or two. His message was accompanied by a list of upcoming training courses, conferences, and symposia surrounding bat rescue and care. She made a mental note to attend a couple that sounded particularly relevant to her.

Harriet greeted Polly when she arrived and decided to enjoy her second cup of coffee on the patio. But before she could pour it, the office phone rang. Polly answered it and then called Harriet to the phone. It was Jane Birtwhistle.

"Good morning, Jane. How are you today?" Harriet said, wondering if Mittens or one of the woman's other cats needed immediate medical attention. She could hardly wait to share the good news about the relocated sea chest with her. But that would have to wait. Vet business first.

"Oh, Harriet, thank you so much. My figurines are back," Jane gushed. Her voice was high-pitched with excitement. "I found the box on the doorstep this morning. Wherever did you find them, Harriet? And how can I ever thank you? You're a dear!"

Harriet was speechless. Had Will reneged on his agreement to allow her to notify Jane about the seamen's chest in the church crypts?

CHAPTER TWENTY-ONE

Harriet arrived at Jane's cottage as soon as she could. The elderly woman greeted her warmly and repeated her startling announcement. "Some of my family's Staffordshire figurines have been returned." A faint blush bloomed on her wrinkled cheeks. Her blue eyes glistened with unshed tears. "I don't know where you found them, Harriet, or how. It doesn't matter, truly. I'm just so grateful to have them back. Come see."

"Jane, I had nothing to do with them being returned," Harriet confessed, following her into the parlor. She felt confused and disappointed that Will hadn't let her call Jane about the figurines after all. Had he been too eager to return the items to her as soon as possible?

For a moment, Jane looked as puzzled as Harriet felt. "You had nothing to do with this?" She made a sweeping gesture, indicating an empty cardboard box on the coffee table surrounded by an assortment of Staffordshire figurines. Clumps of straw—apparently used as packing material—dotted the table. Harriet could smell the tang of old dust in the air and a slightly pungent odor too. Mothballs, perhaps?

"Was there a note inside the box? Did you receive a phone call from Pastor Will that the figurines would be returned?" Harriet asked.

Jane frowned. "Pastor Will? He didn't call, and there was no note in the box. I opened the door this morning to let the cats out and found it on the doorstep. You could have knocked me over with a feather when I lifted the lid and saw what was inside. I was that surprised."

"I'm surprised you were able to bring it inside," Harriet said. "Wasn't it rather heavy?"

"Oh, I wasn't, dear," Jane told her. "I left the box on the doorstep and brought two figures in at a time. Then when the box was nearly empty, I carried it inside." She picked up a fanciful porcelain sheep and tipped it over to show Harriet. "See? This was my mother's. There's the little dot of nail polish on the bottom. Was Pastor Will supposed to call me? Is he the one who found them?"

Harriet studied the figurines on the low table before her. She didn't know what to say. Had Will repacked the figurines into this box? Not one of them represented a woman seated on a horse. Hadn't he said he'd found one like that in the old sea chest? Why hadn't he returned it along with the others?

Frowning, she said, "Yesterday Pastor Will told me that he and Ronnie Reynolds discovered some crates and an old sea chest in one of the crypts. The chest contained a letter written by your mother, so he knew the figurines belonged to you. There was a silver spoon inside too."

"I didn't find a spoon inside the box, or a letter." Heaving a sigh, Jane sank down on the love seat. She slumped, as though overcome by the excitement of her unexpected discovery. "I'm thrilled. To have some of Mum's figurines returned to me after all this time—it's amazing. I'm so thankful. In her journal, she mentioned something about my grandfather hiding the sea chest at the church. I guess Pastor Will found that."

Harriet felt a surge of conflicting emotions. On the one hand, she was delighted that her friend had gotten some of her property restored. On the other hand, she was puzzled that Will had returned them before she'd had time to share the good news with Jane. And where was the figurine of the woman on the horse? Was it possible that these figurines were not the ones Will had discovered?

She picked up an elegant greyhound, admiring the craftsmanship. "I'm confused. I'm not sure these are the ones Will found."

Jane took a handkerchief from the pocket of her floral shirt dress and dabbed at her eyes. "Really? Well, I'm overcome, Harriet. Simply overcome with joy." She smiled through her tears. "You've denied having anything to do with their return, but I know you must be responsible in some way. How could you not be? You brought me the King Charles spaniel after all, and I'm more grateful than I can say."

Harriet arched an eyebrow. "Believe me, Jane, I had nothing to do with this." She indicated the figurines on the coffee table. "But I'm happy for you. And if I'm not mistaken, your collection will soon be complete. I honestly don't think these are the figurines Will found in the old sea chest. As you said, there's no silver spoon or letter here."

Jane scooped up one of her cats and cradled it. "But they must be. How else do you explain it?"

"I can't," Harriet confessed. She opened her mouth to tell Jane that she hadn't told anyone about returning the little King Charles spaniel figurine that Randy had given to her. But then she realized that wasn't true. She'd mentioned it to Will and Doreen. And probably Polly and Aunt Jinny too.

Harriet pressed her lips into a thin, grim line. Now she remembered, she'd told Ava that the figurine Randy had given her originally belonged to Jane. She'd also mentioned to Ava that Jane would like to have the rest of the figurines returned to her, that they had great sentimental value. Was Ava responsible for seeing that the missing porcelain pieces were left on Jane's doorstep? If so, where on earth had they been found?

Was it possible that Ava and Randy had discovered the other figurines in a crate in a smugglers' tunnel after all these years? If so, and they'd decided to return them to Jane, how had they managed to do so? Ava and Randy and Gabriel were all too young to drive, so they couldn't have transported the figurines to Jane's house that way. Had they delivered them on their bikes in the wee hours of the morning? Surely not. The figurines were too fragile. That meant they must have recruited someone with access to a vehicle to deliver the box to Jane. But what adult would have agreed to the secrecy?

Had Ava known all along who had the figurines? Had she convinced that person to return them to Jane? Perhaps she'd told her parents about it and either Doreen or Tom had secretly delivered the box. But that wasn't like the Danbys at all. They would have made a point of returning the figurines directly to Jane herself, probably with fresh scones, if Harriet knew Doreen. Possibilities buzzed around Harriet's brain like a swarm of bees. One thing she knew for sure was that she had to speak with Randy and Ava right away. No more procrastinating.

Lifting the empty cardboard container, Harriet said, "This is not the original box your mother put the figurines in, is it?"

"No, my grandfather and Mum used a wooden crate from the greengrocer," Jane explained. "She wrote the details in her journal. And Mum said there were other things in the crate and the sea chest as well. I'm so flustered, I can't remember what they were. I should reread her journal and refresh my memory." She made a fluttery gesture with her hands then smiled when Mittens rubbed his head against her fingers. "I don't know what to say. I want to thank someone—no, I *need* to thank someone for returning these to me. I never thought I'd see them for myself, and they were so important to Mum."

Harriet lifted a curious orange cat from the table, placed the squirming animal on the floor, and studied the figurines. She'd thought the same thing, that Jane might never see the figurines after all this time. But here they were, apparently no worse for wear. "They aren't damaged, are they?"

Jane shook her head. "Not a crack or chip among the lot." She fixed a hopeful gaze on Harriet's face. "Does this mean the rest of my belongings will be returned too, the other items that were packed away with these?"

"I have no idea," Harriet said. "It probably depends on where these came from."

"Do sit down, Harriet," Jane urged. "You're making me nervous. I don't know what to do next. If someone went to all the trouble to recover these, I may owe them something. Do you think they found them for sale somewhere? Surely they haven't been in the smugglers' tunnel all these years. Word would have gotten around town that other boxes, crates, and chests have been found. Don't you think so?"

Harriet sat down beside her on the love seat and placed a reassuring hand on the woman's frail shoulder. "I don't know, Jane. But I will certainly look into it. We'll figure this out."

"It's all so curious. I don't know what to think," Jane said.

Harriet didn't know what to think either. She wouldn't mention her conversation with Ava, not now. She'd explained to the girl how Jane's mother had marked each figure on the bottom and hidden them away during the war so the Nazis wouldn't get their hands on the family's prized possessions.

Harriet's explanation must have touched a chord in Ava's soft heart, and then Ava talked her younger brother into returning the rest of the figurines to Jane. Had the kids discovered the secret stash in a tunnel? If so, where was the rest of it?

Harriet was still pondering the possible answers to these questions later that evening when she and Will enjoyed a brisk stroll along the bluffs. The evening weather was delightful. She could hear the screech of gulls in the distance as she squeezed Will's hand and told him how some of Jane Birtwhistle's figurines had been returned anonymously.

"But they aren't the ones I found," Will said, clearly astonished. "You said you wanted to call her with the good news, and I've been waiting for you to get back to me."

"That's what I thought," Harriet told him. "So the ones she found on her doorstep this morning came from the crate, the one hidden in a smugglers' tunnel."

"Another mystery," Will said. "You seem to attract them like a magnet. Any idea who the kind benefactor is?"

"I don't know. I could make a guess, but I'm not sure I'd be right—or at least, not completely right," she confessed.

"Go on then."

"Randy and Ava Danby must have discovered them," Harriet said. "According to the journal Jane's mother kept during the war, she and her father stashed their treasures in two separate containers. Jane's grandfather hid one at the church—the one you found, apparently, and the other in a tunnel somewhere."

"Why don't you start from the beginning and recap the story for me?" Will said.

And so she did, starting with the morning the week before when Randy presented her with the whimsical figurine and ending with the discovery of the recovered figurines left on Jane's doorstep.

"Sooner or later you're going to have to speak with Ava and Randy," Will said, stroking his chin pensively.

"I meant to do it before this. Maybe you should come with me," Harriet said hopefully. "We might have to include Gabriel Mellon in the conversation too. I can't believe he doesn't have something to do with all of it."

"Why do you think Gabriel is involved?"

"Doreen told me that Randy is practically living in Gabriel's pocket this summer, so I'm sure they're in this together—whatever *this* is." Harriet tossed her ponytail over her shoulder. "What really puzzles me is how the box of figurines ended up on Jane's front step this morning. The kids can't drive, and I can't picture them pedaling through town with the figurines strapped to the back of a bicycle."

"Maybe the kids just carried the box to Jane's house."

"But from where?" Harriet pressed. "A tunnel? Or did someone else discover the contents of the tunnel and pile them in a heap somewhere? Randy told his mom he found the dog figurine in a box of rubbish. I need to get him to tell me where he found the box."

Will squeezed her hand. "Jane's figurines have been returned, and I'll see that she gets the remainder of them at once. All's well that ends well, right?"

"Not exactly," Harriet went on. "What happened to the other things inside the original crate that Jane's mother packed away? If Ava and Randy found the actual crate, why not return that too? Why take the figurines out and repack them in a cardboard box?"

The corners of Will's mouth turned down. "Maybe you should hand the matter over to Van. This could be a case for the police."

Harriet shook her head adamantly. "Oh, I couldn't. At least, not yet. I need to speak with the kids before I do that. And my hands are tied in a way because I promised Ava I wouldn't bring up the subject with her parents—although that promise came with an expiration date that might be fast approaching."

"Looks like you've gotten yourself in a pickle, sweetheart," Will said.

"I know." She sighed heavily. "I really need to speak with Doreen again about this. Maybe I can keep the kids' names out of it somehow."

Harriet felt depressed. What kind of friend and neighbor was she anyway? What if the Danby kids were in trouble—real trouble— and she had been keeping their secret?

As if he'd read her mind, Will said, "You know, Harriet, you'll never forgive yourself if Ava and Randy get in trouble with the authorities over this and the Danbys find out you kept your suspicions to yourself. How would you feel if you were in their shoes—Tom's and Doreen's, I mean?"

"I see your point." Furthermore, what if someone found the kids' stash, declared it stolen property, and brought charges against them? She had to tell Doreen what she knew and soon. "I'll speak with Doreen. But if I do and she tells Ava, Ava will never trust me again."

"And if Ava and Randy get hurt, Doreen and Tom may never forgive you either. Do you realize that the kids might have discovered the old smugglers' tunnel where the goods were stashed during the war? All of those items should be returned to their proper homes."

"That would explain Randy's secrecy and also Ava's unwillingness to spill the beans."

"What happens if the tunnel collapses or floods?" Will went on. "The kids could be in physical danger. They could get trapped."

Harriet shuddered. "Will you come with me to speak with Doreen?"

Will squeezed her hand. "Of course, but I can't this evening. How about tomorrow evening? There's choir practice, but I can easily get someone else to open the church and lock up afterward. Let's plan on it."

"As much as I'd feel better with you there, I need to talk to Doreen tonight," Harriet said. "But speaking of tomorrow, I need to take the injured owl over to a wildlife rehab center. Would you like to come with me for that in the morning? If the weather is as fine as it was today, it'll be a lovely drive. We can stop for lunch somewhere on our way back."

"Is it one of the centers you've used in the past?"

"No, unfortunately. They're full. However, Garth was able to recommend another center he works with frequently, and he's let them know I'll drop the owl off tomorrow."

"I think I'm free," Will said. "I'll check my calendar and have Claire confirm my schedule to see if I'm able to get away. I'll drive."

"Why?" Harriet demanded with mock resentment. "I know how to drive on the wrong side of the road now—I mean the *left* side of the road." She gave him a teasing sidelong glance.

"It's not that. I'm not chugging along the motorway in that old beast of your grandfather's," Will told her, grinning. "It'll jar the teeth right out of my head."

Harriet laughed, grateful for the moment of levity. She doubted she would have many of those when she went to talk to Doreen.

CHAPTER TWENTY-TWO

Harriet called Doreen as soon as she returned to the house. It was time to sit down with the kids and get to the bottom of what was going on.

Doreen picked up on the second ring, sounding out of breath. "Danby residence. This is Doreen."

"Hi, Doreen. It's Harriet."

Doreen's voice brightened. "Hello, Harriet. What can I do for you, neighbor?"

Feeling like a thorough traitor, Harriet decided to get right to the point. "I was wondering if I could swing by and have a talk with you, Ava, and Randy. I feel as if I've let things go on too long with the figurine, and I want to resolve them. Today, if possible."

"Oh," Doreen said quietly. "As much as I agree with you about a prompt resolution, I'm afraid it's not possible at the moment."

"What do you mean?"

"Ava and Randy aren't here right now. Ava is babysitting and won't be back until late. Randy is spending the night with a friend."

Harriet sighed, almost too frustrated for words. "I understand. I don't know why I thought their summer schedules would be easier to coordinate. Will you let me know when would be a good time to do this? I think it's important that we get it taken care of as soon as we can."

"I agree," Doreen replied. "I'll call you, okay?"

"Okay." Harriet said good night and ended the call.

Later that evening, as she lay in bed trying—and failing—to keep her attention on a mystery novel, she finally set her book down and switched off the bedside lamp.

Then she tossed and turned all night.

At lunchtime the next day, Harriet and Will were seated at a table by a window in the charming dining room of the Quill and Scroll. They'd ordered hearty roast beef sandwiches and a Bakewell tart for dessert.

The drive to the wildlife rehab center had been as lovely as Harriet had predicted. The facility was clean and well run, the staff veterinarian friendly and competent. Harriet felt reassured that the injured owl would be well cared for and released back into the wild when he was ready.

As she raised her glass of water to her lips, Harriet glanced around the crowded dining room. Business was booming. The Beems must be pleased.

Suddenly, she sat straight up. "Will, you'll never believe who's seated at the table in the far corner near the kitchen. But don't look."

"Who is it then?" he wanted to know.

Harriet felt a low, ominous stirring of misgiving. "Nettie Mackenzie."

Will's eyebrow rose sharply. "Are you sure?"

Harriet nodded, remembering her own suggestion to Celia that if someone was trying to sabotage the inn, they should be more forceful. One of her ideas had been for the saboteur to damage the inn's reputation by releasing rats in the kitchen. Was it only a coincidence that Nettie was seated near the kitchen? Had she requested that table? Harriet craned her neck, trying to see if Nettie had brought a large tote bag, satchel, or some other container convenient for carrying something unsavory.

"What's she doing?" Will asked.

"Eating something. One of those soft sweet rolls Polly calls a Bath bun, I think. And she has a cup of tea." Harriet noted that the middle-aged pub owner sat stiff and rigid in her chair as though she'd suffered a back injury. Or maybe she was uncomfortable in enemy territory, so to speak. Her brown hair was disheveled, her pale blue shirt rumpled. She didn't look happy.

Celia bustled into the dining room, spotted Will and Harriet, and made her way to their table. Unlike the waitstaff in their neat black slacks and crisp white shirts, Celia wore a hot-pink sleeveless dress with ruffles at the throat and a slender sash at the waist. She presented the pretty picture of the perfect hostess in sharp contrast to Nettie, who'd greeted them with brusque hostility when they'd dined at the Pint Pot.

"Harriet, Will, it's so nice to see you again," Celia chirped. "I hope you're finding everything to your satisfaction."

"Most definitely," Will assured her.

"Everything is perfect," Harriet said. She lowered her voice. "And I notice you have a special guest this afternoon. Over in the corner near the kitchen."

Celia gave a short, self-conscious laugh. "Trust me—I know. You could have knocked me over with a feather when she strolled in, bold as brass."

"Did she request that table?" Harriet asked.

"No. I seated her myself." Celia glanced over her shoulder. "I know many people don't like to be seated near the kitchen because of the noise and bustle, but she told me she'd come to look the place over now that it was open for business. I guessed that she'd poke her head into the parlor and meander upstairs too. She might as well sit near the kitchen so she can inspect that as well before she goes."

Thinking it wise to change the subject, Harriet asked, "How's Scarlett? Is her skin condition clearing up? Is she responding well to the medication?"

Before Celia could reply, Nettie approached their table with a frosty expression for Will and Harriet. But her voice was almost pleasant when she addressed Celia. "Mrs. Beem, I've been an old stick. You have a very nice establishment here. I was worried that you'd be taking away my customers. Owning a business is hard enough without competition. But I can see your place appeals to the upper crust. Lots of tourists too, from the looks of things. My regulars wouldn't feel comfortable here. Good luck to you." Without waiting for a response, Nettie walked away, heading for the checkout counter to pay her tab.

"Well, I never!" Celia declared. "I can't tell whether I'm flattered by the compliments or offended that anyone might feel uncomfortable in my inn."

Will and Harriet exchanged surprised glances but remained silent. What could they say? Now it was clear that Nettie wasn't trying to drive the Beems out of business. She had just confirmed that the Pint Pot and the Quill and Scroll weren't competing for the same demographic.

Before Harriet could express this thought aloud to their hostess, Celia was called to the telephone by a young waitress.

"Will wonders never cease," Will murmured, returning his attention to his sandwich.

Harriet silently agreed.

They were nearly through with their meal when Celia approached their table again, a strange expression of fear and excitement on her flushed face. Clutching Harriet by the wrist, she gasped, "Come with me right now. You can hear the voices in the parlor."

Will rose quickly. Harriet did the same. She could hardly help it as Celia, still clutching her wrist in a fierce grip, practically dragged her to the parlor.

Leading them toward the bench near the fireplace, she whispered hoarsely, "Listen. Do you hear that?" She pointed an accusing finger at the wall behind the bench.

Harriet strained to listen. "I do hear something," she said. "Sounds like mumbling." Turning to Will, she asked, "Do you hear it too?"

Will nodded. He regarded the bench and the wall behind it. "Definitely people talking, but I can't make out what they're saying. Can you?"

Harriet shook her head. "No, I can't distinguish any words. I'm not even sure whether the voices are male or female."

"I told you!" Celia's tone held a note of triumph. "I didn't imagine all this. You finally hear it too. Where is it coming from? What are we going to do about it?"

With a frown, Harriet asked, "Is someone in the cellar? Where's Freddie?"

"He took Scarlett for a walk along the beach," Celia said. "There's no one in the cellar. There can't be. We've been keeping the door locked."

"And besides, we've checked down there more than once," Will reminded them. "There's no secret entrance or anything of that nature. I'm sure of that."

"What's going on in here?" demanded a sharp voice.

Harriet, Will, and Celia whirled toward the doorway.

Nettie stood there with a puzzled frown. "You dashed in here so quickly, I thought there might be a fire or some other emergency. What's happening?"

Deciding that honesty was the best policy, Harriet replied, "We're trying to find out where some mysterious noises are coming from."

Nettie gave her a dubious stare and folded her arms across her chest. After a long moment of uncomfortable silence, she drawled, "If you say so."

Just then, the grate rattled noisily. This was followed by what seemed to be muted laughter. Nettie's eyebrows shot up. "What on earth was that?"

Celia raised her chin. "That's what we're trying to figure out."

"Someone in your cellar?" Nettie suggested, walking into the room.

"No," Celia replied. "There's no way someone could be down there right now."

Harriet stepped closer to the fireplace before turning her attention to the storage bench again. "We tried moving this before, didn't we, looking for a secret passageway?"

"Yes, but it's built right into the wall." Celia gave the bench a hard yank to demonstrate. It didn't budge.

Harriet pursed her lips. There was no mistake. She'd heard voices and laughter. It seemed to be coming from inside the bench. An icy finger of fear tickled her spine.

Celia pointed at the fireplace. "That's what I've been hearing. The voices are bad enough, but when the grate begins to rattle like that, it scares me to death. I feel like the old inn is going to come tumbling down around my ears, but the building inspectors—both of them—have assured me that no such thing will happen."

"The building and the chimney are sound?" Nettie asked.

Celia gave a curt nod. Harriet sensed that she was not pleased to have Nettie in the parlor with them, but she probably didn't know how to ask her to leave without sounding rude, especially since Nettie had just made an attempt to improve their relationship.

Harriet cast Will a mute appeal for help.

He gave her a small nod. "All right, there must be a hidden passageway or a priest hole behind these walls somewhere." He began tapping the walls with his knuckles, listening for hollow spaces. Harriet recalled the Clutterbuck brothers doing the same without result. "Would you like to lend a hand, Mrs. Mackenzie?"

Nettie blinked once or twice, obviously taken aback by his question. Then her face brightened. "Absolutely. Wouldn't it be exciting to discover an old priest hole?" She began knocking on the adjacent wall.

"What exactly is a priest hole?" Harriet asked.

"It was a hiding place for Roman Catholic priests during times of religious persecution," Will explained. "Fairly common in old homes and inns like this one."

Freddie entered the room with Scarlett at his heels. "What's all this?" With a cautious glance at his wife and an even more cautious one at Nettie, he asked, "Hearing voices again?"

Celia folded her arms across her chest. "We all heard the voices and the grate rattling. No one can blame either on a summer storm or a strong wind causing the timbers to creak."

"Can't blame the drains either," Nettie chimed in. "I've had trouble with drains out at the Pint Pot. I know what that sounds like. This is different."

Suddenly, Harriet thought she heard an angry shout coming from inside the storage bench. Before she could second-guess herself, Scarlett lunged at the bench, barking and growling.

"We've already looked inside the bench," Celia said, eyeing her dog's behavior.

"Perhaps we didn't look hard enough," Harriet suggested. She lifted the lid and removed the maps, brochures, and magazines scattered at the bottom. She handed them to Nettie, who hovered eagerly at her elbow. The empty bench now revealed a deep, well-varnished bottom that Harriet began exploring.

When she discovered indentations on the floor of the bench, she announced with a thrill of excitement, "There's something here."

"What is it?" Will asked, drawing nearer.

"It's a set of grooves. Maybe this is a false bottom." Harriet dug her fingers into the grooves and pulled. The varnished board lifted out of the bench. Harriet handed it to Will as the others murmured with surprise. Then Harriet peered into the bench, and her throat went dry. "I see stairs."

Celia clapped her hands over her mouth, and Freddie put an arm around her waist.

Will and Nettie leaned over the bench, staring down into the darkness. "Now where does that go, I wonder?" Nettie asked, her eyes alight with excitement.

"Your guess is as good as mine," Freddie replied.

"May we borrow a torch or two?" Will asked their hosts.

"I'll get them. Are you all right, dear?" Freddie asked his wife.

Celia's face was pale, but she nodded.

Freddie dashed out of the room.

Scarlett continued to growl at the bench.

Harriet took Celia's elbow gently, asking in a low voice, "Can you take Scarlett out of the room? We don't want to scare whoever's down there away."

"Right." Celia seized Scarlett's collar and took the dog out. When she returned with Freddie at her side, they shut the door of the parlor behind them.

For a moment, they all crowded around the bench. Harriet could still hear two or three voices. She couldn't be sure, as they were too faint to distinguish clearly. She clasped Will's hand, and he squeezed it.

The others stood mute and obviously stunned.

Mustering her courage, Harriet took one of the flashlights from Freddie. "I'm going down," she whispered.

"Not without me," Will replied, taking the flashlight from her.

Harriet could feel the sweat on her palms and the rapid pace of her pulse. But her curiosity was stronger than her fear. For a brief moment she wished Van were here with them. After all, the intruders below might be part of the gang of criminals who'd been stealing car parts. Or worse.

"I'll go first," Will said. He aimed the beam of the flashlight down into the yawning cavity. "Watch your step, Harriet. It's quite narrow, and so are the steps."

Harriet watched Will carefully disappear into the darkness below. Then it was her turn. The stairs reminded her of the sort of ladder one used to climb into an upper bunk. She descended slowly, cautiously, mindful of the faces peering down at her from above.

When she and Will reached the bottom, they discovered a heavy wooden door with an old-fashioned white porcelain doorknob. "What do you make of this?" Will whispered, shining the light all around.

"I haven't a clue," she replied. "It's odd, to say the least. But I guess this is your priest's hole. And a good hiding place it is too, since we had no clue it was here when we explored the cellar." Harriet twisted the doorknob, but it didn't move. "It must be locked."

"Let me try." Will gripped the knob and rattled it hard. The door didn't budge.

Suddenly, he stopped, placing a finger on his lips.

She strained to listen. Now she could hear whispering. There were people on the other side of the door, and those people knew she and Will were there.

She heard the sound of a lock clicking. The door began to open slowly—very slowly.

Harriet caught her breath and clutched at Will's hand, grasping it hard. He gave her a reassuring squeeze. With her other hand, she gripped the flashlight firmly in case she needed to use it to defend herself from whoever was on the other side of the door.

The door opened wider.

Harriet saw a short, vaguely familiar figure standing there in the gloom.

Will raised the flashlight.

The figure exclaimed, "It's Doc Bailey and the pastor! We're in for it now."

CHAPTER TWENTY-THREE

Will pushed against the creaking door, opening it even farther.

Randy Danby, wide-eyed and mouth agape, took a faltering step back to allow Harriet and Will to enter the dimly lit chamber. Battery-powered camping lanterns cast odd shadows against the walls. A narrow central pathway was lined with half-opened crates, barrels, and assorted trunks and boxes. Several of these had been examined rather thoroughly, judging by the amount of straw and wood shavings all around.

One of the open crates clearly bore the name *Florence Birtwhistle*.

Randy was not alone. Gabriel stood directly behind him, clutching a pry bar in one hand and glowering at them. Ava was there too, and so was seventeen-year-old Thommy Danby.

Harriet felt a rush of alarm. "What in the world is going on here?"

The youngsters all began talking at once.

"Doc Harriet, we didn't steal any of this, honest," Randy said, his voice quavering. "We were just playing pirates."

"Finders keepers!" Gabriel bellowed.

Ava chimed in, "We should have said something to Mum and Dad as soon as we found this stuff."

"That's what I told you to do." Thommy's tan cheeks flushed with embarrassment. "I can just imagine what you're thinking," he added to Will and Harriet.

"What are we thinking?" Will asked, his tone calm and measured.

That seemed to catch all four off guard.

Finally, Thommy said, "You think these are stolen goods, but that's not true. The kids found this stuff down here. They opened some of the boxes, as you can see. But they didn't steal anything."

Harriet glanced around the narrow chamber. It smelled damp, old, and somewhat salty. "How did you kids find this place?"

"Through that massive old wardrobe in Mrs. Coomb's house, like you read about in the books," Randy told her. "That's Gabriel's grandmother. She lives next door."

"The floor of the wardrobe lifts out, and there are steps that go into that room." Gabriel pointed to another door behind Thommy, who stood with his arms folded across his chest.

"And there's a real, honest-to-goodness smugglers' cave off that room," Randy went on, his voice tinged with excitement. "And tunnels off that. We could walk right on through to the beach if there hadn't been a cave-in."

Harriet could tell he was thrilled by the adventure of it all. What boy his age wouldn't be?

"You'll have to give all of this to the people it belongs to," Will told Gabriel. His tone was kind, but firm. "As you can see, the boxes and crates have been clearly identified with names."

"No way," Gabriel snapped, his icy gaze drilling into Will and Harriet.

"I was hoping this was really pirate loot, and the names were the people the pirates stole from," Randy said, shoulders slouching. He looked at Harriet, his eyes reflecting his keen disappointment. "I figured those people were long gone by now, so they'd never miss it."

"Even if that were the case, it's our duty to find the original owners' descendants and at least offer their family heirlooms back to them," Harriet said.

"I told you," Thommy snarled.

"Besides, it's not pirate loot." Harriet went on to explain how the Birtwhistles and other families in the community had hidden their personal belongs to protect them from being confiscated by the Nazis during World War II.

Randy flung an angry glare at Gabriel. "*He* said pirates stashed this stuff here."

Ava jabbed her younger brother in the ribs with a sharp elbow. "I told you that wasn't true, Randy. See the names?" She pointed to a battered footlocker with the name *Trumble* painted on the top. "And Miss B's old figurines were down here too. Those weren't stolen by pirates." She snorted with disgust before casting a withering glance in Gabriel's direction. Perhaps the summer crush was over. If so, Doreen would be pleased.

"Speaking of Miss Birtwhistle, who returned the figurines to her?" Harriet asked.

"That was me." Thommy came forward, careful not to step on the various items strewn across the floor. "I borrowed Dad's pickup and delivered them to her cottage. Ava said I needed to do it secretly. I didn't like the sound of that, so I knew they were up to something. I could tell those figurines were valuable. Staffordshire, right?" He shifted his weight from one leg to the other. "I made Ava bring me down here to see what's been going on, and I'm glad she did."

"I didn't want to," Ava said. "But it didn't feel right."

Will said, "You did the right thing returning those items to Miss Birtwhistle. She was delighted to have them back. They've been missing for over eighty years, you know."

Gabriel had fallen silent. His frown had disappeared. He stared at the assorted boxes and crates with a blank expression on his face.

"What are you thinking?" Harriet asked him.

With a sullen shrug, Gabriel said, "I just wanted to have some fun this summer. An adventure." He shifted the pry bar from one hand to the other and cast a glance at the Danby kids.

"I'll take that," Will said, holding out his hand for the pry bar.

Gabriel surrendered it to him.

"All of you will be responsible for seeing that these things are returned to their rightful owners," Will went on. "I'm sure they'll be as delighted to have their family's treasures returned as Miss Birtwhistle is."

The door behind Harriet opened even wider with a loud creak. Surprised, she turned to see Nettie and Freddie standing on the threshold.

"What's all this?" Freddie demanded, a look of utter astonishment on his face.

Nettie, on the other hand, looked thrilled. Her cheeks were flushed, her eyes bright, her features more animated than Harriet had ever seen them. "It's true! There *is* an old smugglers' cave under the inn."

Harriet and Will stepped aside, allowing the two newcomers to come farther into the crowded chamber.

"This isn't the cave," Gabriel grumbled. "The cave is that way." He pointed to the half-open door behind Thommy.

"And these aren't smuggled goods either," Harriet added. "During World War II, some of the families in the village hid their more precious belongings down here to protect them from the Nazis."

Nettie nodded. "My grandad told me something about that."

"We need to deliver all this stuff," Freddie said. "As soon as we can. I guess I should notify the police too."

"I can help," Nettie volunteered. "I recognize some of the names, so I'll be able to point you in the right direction."

Freddie moved into the middle of the room, careful to avoid stepping on anything of value. "We'll have to carry these things up to the parlor. I don't want the families to come down here themselves to claim their belongings. Someone could trip and fall on the stairs. I don't want anyone to get hurt."

Harriet turned to Gabriel. "Perhaps you'd like to show Pastor Will the old wardrobe in your grandmother's house. Depending on how wide that opening is, it might be wiser to move the goods through there."

"Does your grandmother know you found the secret stairway inside the old wardrobe?" Will asked.

Gabriel ducked his head. "I didn't tell her."

"So she doesn't know what you've been up to?" Thommy demanded.

"Of course not. She'd have put a stop to all our fun," Gabriel said.

"I'll show you, Pastor Will," Randy volunteered. "The wardrobe is in a spare bedroom that doesn't get used much. Mrs. Coomb stores things in there like old furniture, all covered with sheets."

"I want to see the smugglers' cave," Nettie insisted. "I've heard about them all my life. Will someone show me the way?"

"You won't see much," Gabriel told her. "Randy and I tried to get through, but there must have been a cave-in or flood or something a long time ago. It's blocked off with all sorts of rocks and beams and stuff." He eyed Nettie skeptically. "You'd never get through."

"I'll show you the entrance to it, ma'am," Ava volunteered. "You won't want to go in, though. There are puddles and wet clay everywhere, and it's messy. You'll ruin your shoes."

"Must have been a jolly good hiding place back in the day," Randy added. "It goes all the way to the beach, I think." He faced Harriet with an inquisitive expression. "Hey, how did you all know we were here? Where did you come from anyhow?"

Harriet grinned. "There's a secret staircase in the storage bench in the inn's parlor. Rather like the one in that old wardrobe next door, I imagine."

"You don't say!" Randy exclaimed.

"We've suspected someone's been down here for quite a while," Freddie added. "Sometimes, we heard your voices. Other times, the grate would jump. It made quite a racket."

Thommy pointed to the old door behind him. "That thing makes a loud clang when you shut it all the way. It's heavier than it looks. I suppose it could rattle the grate upstairs."

Freddie chuckled. "Wait until Celia hears about this. She'll be so relieved we don't have ghosts after all. Nothing but a bunch of kids going through loot hidden from the Nazis."

"You thought we were ghosts?" Randy asked, puzzled.

"They didn't know about the secret stairs. They heard voices with no apparent source," Harriet told him, grinning. The mystery had been solved. She could hardly wait to tell Polly and Aunt Jinny. What Tom and Doreen would think when they learned about this, she couldn't imagine, but at least it seemed that no real harm had been done. In fact, the kids' adventures were likely to lead to a great service in the form of people being reunited with their ancestors' things. Not that returning the items to the rightful owners would be an easy task.

"Come along now. I thought someone was showing me the entrance to the cave." Nettie headed toward the opposite door, picking up one of the glowing lanterns as she did so.

Freddie followed her. "That's strange to me. If there's a cave, why bother with these secret storage rooms? Couldn't the smugglers simply hide the goods in the cave?"

"I can guess," Nettie told him. "Caves are wet and messy, as this girl rightly pointed out." She gestured to Ava. "Depending on what sort of goods you're smuggling, they could become water-damaged, which kind of defeats the purpose. No one's going to pay for damaged goods. These rooms are dry and almost cozy. Items that are sensitive to damp would be safe here."

Ava nodded vigorously. "The lady's right. We saw something that looked like bolts of cloth along one wall. They were rotted and falling apart."

"Might have been silk that's moldered away. They smuggled that back in the day," Nettie said.

"The king's excise men were quite savvy about locating caves. After all, you can see a lot of them in the cliff face," Will added. "The smugglers had to be savvy too. They built secret storage chambers like this one, connected to the cave by a hidden door. That way when the king's men showed up, they wouldn't find anything inside the cave."

"And as you showed, Mr. Beem, even if the excise men could hear the smugglers moving around down here, they wouldn't necessarily be able to find the entrance to the room," Thommy said. "Though I have to believe the smugglers would know to be absolutely silent."

"Follow me. I'll show you what you want to see," Gabriel said, seemingly eager now. He stepped past Ava to lead the way.

As they followed the boy into the next room, Will moved his flashlight over the walls. To Freddie, he said, "Pretty amazing construction, don't you think? We explored your cellar more than once and never suspected hidden rooms down here on the other side of the cellar walls."

"Never did," Freddie agreed. "Mighty clever, I'd say. I suppose their lives depended on being quick and clever."

Gabriel led them to the far wall of the second chamber and pointed. "That leads to the cave."

Will and Harriet focused their beams on a suspicious spot on the wall. To Harriet, it didn't look like a door. It was rough, gray, and rather like a lumpy patch job.

Gabriel ran his hands over the grimy surface. His fingers caught on something, and he pulled. With a loud *clunk*, the camouflaged door opened to reveal the entrance to the infamous smugglers' cave.

Nettie laughed with delight. Raising her lantern, she peered through the dark, rather ominous opening.

Harriet did the same. She first noted the air of abandonment, the musty smell. It was chilly, and she could hear the faint sound of dripping in the distance. The passageway looked narrow and twisting.

"Watch out for the puddles," Ava warned.

"There might be a drop-off," Thommy cautioned.

"I'm not going in," Harriet assured them. "I just wanted to have a peek."

"Look at that." Nettie raised the light, revealing broken stalactites hanging from the ceiling. To one side, there was a crude wooden table, now collapsed with age. Bolts of shredded cloth tumbled from it, and several empty bottles were clustered around.

"Think of the tales this old cave could tell," Harriet murmured.

"Yes, if only caves could talk," Nettie added wistfully.

An hour later, they all mingled in the parlor, partaking of the refreshments that Celia had cheerfully provided. She offered tea and coffee for the adults and orange squash for the kids with plenty of assorted biscuits and little cream cakes to go around. Gabriel, Ava, and Randy had been thrilled to enter the parlor through the storage bench. Scarlett had barked excitedly as each of them trooped carefully up the steps through the opening. Celia had fluttered around like a hummingbird, delighted that her mystery had been solved.

Helping herself to a second Jammie Dodger—a British cookie made of strawberry jam sandwiched between shortbread biscuits—Harriet told Randy, "I gave Miss Birtwhistle her dog figurine back. She has its mate on the fireplace mantel in her parlor. It was kind of you to give me a present, Randy, and I did love it, but I thought it was best to return the figurine to its rightful owner."

"I didn't mean to do something wrong. I just thought you'd like the dog." Randy ducked his head, his cheeks pink.

Harriet placed a reassuring hand on his shoulder. "I appreciate your thoughtfulness."

Ava joined them, holding a little plate of miniature lemon cream cakes. "Are you going to tell Mum and Dad about all this, Miss Harriet?"

"I think you should tell them," Harriet replied gently. "It would be better coming from you."

A bark of laughter caught her attention. Will and Freddie were regaling Gabriel and Thommy with tales of their unsuccessful hunt for ghosts in the cellar. Scarlett had attached herself to Gabriel, who stroked the dog behind the ears in an absent sort of way. Harriet believed that dogs were good judges of character, so Scarlett must sense something positive about Gabriel. She wondered if Rand Cromwell, the local dogcatcher, might need some summer help at the pound—feeding the animals and walking the dogs perhaps. She intended to find out.

When Ava pulled Randy toward the table for more refreshments, Harriet noticed that Nettie was animatedly explaining the secret chamber to the Clutterbuck brothers, who expressed their strong desire to see the rooms below for themselves.

Harriet had just finished her second cup of coffee when Will came and touched her elbow. "I hate to drag you away from all the excitement, but I do have to get back to the church."

"I know," Harriet said. "I've had a few texts from Polly wondering when I was coming. It's been rather exciting, hasn't it?"

Will's eyes sparkled. "Exciting indeed. And it's going to be even more exciting this Sunday afternoon."

"What's happening Sunday afternoon?"

He grinned. "The Beems are hosting a tea party right here in the parlor for all the families who hid their belongings in the secret room below. And Nettie has offered to help organize it!"

CHAPTER TWENTY-FOUR

White Church Bay
April 1946

Flory rocked in her chair on the front porch, knitting and watching six-year-old Jane coo over a butterfly that had landed on her finger. Beyond her, Donald walked along the stone wall that edged their property, searching for gaps or other problems to be fixed.

He was having a good day. He hadn't woken in a cold sweat in the middle of the night, gasping about shrapnel and men's screams. The nightmares came less and less often the longer he was home, and Flory prayed that one day, they would never come again.

The months after he'd returned had been the worst. He'd been a shell of the man who had left her years before, and Flory had feared she might never see the man she loved again. She'd cared for him tirelessly, soothing him after the nightmares, reminding him of where he was when he stared around with haunted eyes as if seeing the war again. Gradually, he began to smile, often at his beloved daughter. His calm and humor reemerged as well, but there was a new edge to them, as if he feared that his being home and safe was a dream from which he would wake at any moment.

She truly began to see the old Donald again when her father passed away suddenly. Flory had gone to wake Dad one morning shortly after Donald's return, but he hadn't stirred from his bed. The doctor said he'd had a stroke and passed in his sleep. Flory was grateful that he had gone peacefully, and she tried to keep herself together for Donald and Jane. She didn't know whether she hadn't succeeded as well as she'd hoped, or whether the reality of a death had reassured Donald that he was home. Either way, the love and warmth she remembered so well from before he'd gone to war returned in force, and his recovery after that was rapid.

Now he was almost back to normal. Flory didn't think he would ever be truly the same as he had been, but war had a way of changing a man. Her friends in the Women's Institute murmured about the differences in their own sons, brothers, and husbands, so at least she knew she wasn't alone. For now, she was grateful that he was alive and safe. Far too many others couldn't say the same.

Between running a home in a world rebuilding itself from catastrophe, caring for Donald, raising Jane, and grieving the loss of her father, Flory barely thought of the family treasures that had been so carefully hidden away. She'd suddenly remembered them at Dad's funeral of all places then wondered at herself for thinking of them at such a time. And now, every so often, she idly wondered where Dad had hidden her mother's figurines. But there was always something to do, something more pressing and urgent than trying to track down someone who might have hidden their things with hers.

After all, they were just things. They would keep.

Flory turned her face to the sun, relishing the early spring warmth on her skin. Perhaps someday, when the war was little more than a dark shadow on humanity's collective memory, someone would stumble upon her family's belongings and recognize them for what they were—treasures. Maybe they would return the pieces to her. Or maybe they would take the figurines home and allow them to grace a new mantel, every bit as cherished as they had been by Flory's mother.

Jane giggled at something in the yard, and Flory smiled at her. She had all she needed right here, and she was thankful that God had provided for her so richly.

CHAPTER TWENTY-FIVE

Sunday's tea party at the Quill and Scroll was in full swing when Harriet and Will arrived. It was standing room only in the parlor, but no one complained. Spirits were high, the chatter animated and punctuated with laughter.

Harriet, wearing a fitted denim skirt and crisp white eyelet blouse, scanned the crowded parlor with both surprise and admiration. Celia Beem, resplendent in a flowing yellow dress, had outdone herself. The room was decorated with garlands of British flags. The table seemed to bow beneath the weight of platters and trays of food. Music from World War II played in the background. Harriet vaguely recognized the famous "White Cliffs of Dover," sung by Vera Lynn.

"I daresay this is going to be the most popular social event of the summer," Will commented. Always warm and kind, he mingled with people easily. That was one reason his flock loved him so, Harriet mused.

Harriet felt a flutter of excitement as well as a sense of satisfaction. The mystery of the phantom voices had been solved. Families were being reunited with treasured belongings. There were no bats in the church or the parsonage. All was right with the world.

Doreen squeezed her way through the crowd toward them, carrying a slice of pie on a plate. "What a crush!" she declared with a smile. "I was bowled over when Randy and Ava told me what they'd been up to. And this homity pie is the best I've ever eaten. I must get Celia's recipe."

Harriet peered at the food on her friend's plate. "What is homity pie?"

"Potato pie livened up with onions, leeks, and cheese," Doreen explained. "It was a favorite during World War II, and popular now with vegetarians." She pointed to a few vintage posters on the walls. "Aren't they clever? Those are old advertisements from the war."

Glancing in the direction Doreen pointed, Harriet spotted colorful ads for Cadbury Bournville Cocoa and other products. There were posters with talking potatoes and smiling carrots, and others with slogans like *Win with Tin*. It was remarkable what the Beems had pulled off in such a short time, but Celia told Harriet they hadn't done it alone. Nettie had helped as she'd promised, going above and beyond by managing the guest list, and the Clutterbuck brothers had extended their stay to take part in the festivities.

"Wouldn't have missed it for the world," Michael said. Or was it Matthew? Harriet still couldn't tell the difference between the twins, currently red-faced from the summer heat, who were helping people tote crates and boxes outside to waiting vehicles and smiling all the while. Sergeant Oduba was busy taking photos of the recovered items and making notes on a clipboard.

"What do you think of our little tea party?" Celia asked, coming toward them with a bottle of chilled sparkling cider in each hand. The faint scent of floral perfume surrounded her.

"It's amazing," Harriet said, surveying the chattering crowd. Knowing how word traveled in the small community, she was certain that the event would raise the inn's standing and popularity. Locals would certainly come in for meals and recommend the Quill and Scroll to tourists. "I can't believe how quickly you threw everything together—the food, the decorations, and even the invitations." She wondered if she'd be able to pull off a wedding reception with half as much style and efficiency, even with much more time to organize it.

Will added, "It's delightful to see so many residents making connections with their family histories."

Celia thrust her chin toward Freddie, who chatted with several men, some taking notes. "It seems that a few local and regional newspapers caught wind of the story. I think those men are reporters, here to take photos and receive guided tours of the secret passages. One of those gents came all the way from the Imperial War Museum in London. Hoping to pick up some donations to display, he said. But I won't let him bully anyone out of a family heirloom they really want."

"Good for you," Harriet said, knowing her friend's protective stance would endear her to the community.

"And Nettie has been a godsend, truly," Celia added. "I know I told you about her work with the guest list, but she also brought in a carpenter to shore up those rickety stairs from the bench to the secret chamber, to make sure they're safe to use. She also went down there herself and made a list of all the names on the boxes, crates, and trunks. Then she personally notified the families that their belongings had been found. Some of them didn't even know their families had hidden things away."

"Goodness," Harriet said. "She's been a busy bee."

"You have no idea. She even got the Clutterbuck brothers to bring everything upstairs so it could be claimed. I'm pretty sure she's the one who alerted the newspapers as well. I don't know how we would have managed today without her. I much prefer having her in our corner than against us."

"I want your recipe for homity pie," Doreen told their hostess. "It's the best I've ever tasted."

Celia blushed. "That's high praise coming from an accomplished baker like you. Come to the kitchen with me."

As the two women wove through the throng, Will offered to get Harriet a cup of punch, which she readily agreed to. He disappeared among the crowd, greeting everyone with his usual charm.

Aunt Jinny appeared at her side. "This is quite a squeeze, isn't it?"

"It certainly is," Harriet agreed.

Ava and Randy raced to join them, breathless with excitement. Both youngsters had bright eyes and flushed cheeks. "Guess what? We've had our picture taken for the paper!" Randy exclaimed. "Isn't that something?"

"Me too," Ava chimed in. She wore a pink plaid sundress and strappy sandals, her dark hair in a French braid. "They're writing an article about us. And Gabriel too, of course."

"Playing pirates paid off then," Harriet said, giving them both a wry smile.

With a sheepish grin, Randy replied, "I suppose so, but I've learned my lesson about doing it with other people's stuff."

"I'm glad to hear it. And aren't you happy to be a part of all this?" Harriet indicated the crowded parlor filled with laughing, chatting people. Some had even retrieved tissues from purses or handkerchiefs from pockets to dab at tears of joy.

"It's brilliant," Randy agreed.

Gabriel called to him, and he and Ava dashed away once more. Harriet was glad to see that the friendship seemed to have survived. Hopefully the Danby children would have a positive effect on Gabriel after all. Harriet had a feeling he was already learning about kindness and forgiveness from them.

"They'll be talking about this all summer," Aunt Jinny said.

"For sure," Harriet agreed.

Will returned with her punch and promptly hurried away again to fetch a cup for Aunt Jinny.

"This is all wonderful publicity for the Beems," her aunt observed, echoing Harriet's earlier observations. "I doubt the usual grand opening could have been more successful. They'll be turning away customers or keeping a waiting list. I'm sure the current guests will return, and I know they'll tell their friends. What a turnout!"

"And they deserve every bit of it." Jane Birtwhistle, beaming with joy, approached them. "Harriet, I wanted to let you know that I have all my mother's figurines back now. Pastor Will and DC Worthington returned the ones they found in the church crypts. I can't describe how wonderful it is to have the pieces all together again. If Mum were here, I know she'd be over the moon about it."

A quiet woman with the usual British reserve came forward to introduce herself as Donna Coomb. She looked slightly befuddled by all the excitement. She also seemed pleased that her grandson was being hailed as a local hero. "My great-grandfather once told me about the hiding place beneath our house, but I'd forgotten all about it. I was shocked when Gabriel showed me how to access the secret passageway through the old wardrobe."

Harriet turned her attention then to Gabriel, who was regaling a group of children with his adventures. Neatly attired in jeans and a green dress shirt rolled up at the sleeves, Gabriel was clearly enjoying being the center of attention. After a few moments, with Scarlett at his heels, he left his admirers to help the Clutterbuck brothers and the police sergeant reunite excited families with their long-lost possessions.

Will returned with a second cup of punch just in time to shake hands with local plumber Terry Leaper.

Terry cradled a teacup in his large hands. "I was struck dumb when Nettie Mackenzie called to tell me they'd found a trunk belonging to Mavis White in the old smugglers' cave. She was my great-grandmother. Grandma May, we called her."

More than one curious guest lifted the lid of the old storage bench to peer below. Others swapped hand-me-down tales of the war while reporters from various papers mingled with attendees to record their comments.

"Have you seen Polly or Van?" Harriet asked Will. She'd scanned the room several times and had not yet caught a glimpse of her friend's dark head among the crowd.

"I haven't seen either of them," Aunt Jinny said, sounding startled. "How odd. I would have thought they'd be here for sure."

"They weren't in church this morning either," Will added. "Were they invited?"

"Yes, of course," Harriet replied. "Celia told me so when she called to invite me." She mulled over various possible reasons for their absence. She hoped everything was all right. She checked her phone, certain Polly would have texted her if anything was wrong, but there was no message from her friend.

Before she could pursue the matter further, Nettie Mackenzie's niece, Phoebe, approached them, carrying a silver tray heaped with a variety of sandwiches cut neatly into triangles and squares. Attired in black slacks and a white shirt—the same outfit worn by the Beems' waitstaff, the young woman was elegant and bright-eyed.

"It's nice to see you again, Phoebe," Will greeted her.

Phoebe gave him a shy smile and offered them all a sandwich.

"I'm surprised to see you here," Harriet said, helping herself to one filled with smoked salmon and cream cheese.

With a shrug, Phoebe replied, "My aunt volunteered me to help. I don't mind. This is fun. Aunt Nettie has been so happy ever since she saw that secret chamber. I haven't been down there yet. Dark caves and narrow passageways give me the creeps." She shuddered then smiled. "I'm glad to see her showing so much public spirit."

"It's kind of you to help out today," Will told her.

"I'll be working here regularly," she said. Her thin cheeks flushed with pride. "Mrs. Beem offered me a job."

Harriet arched an eyebrow. "How does Aunt Nettie feel about that?"

"She's all for it. She said I need to make my way up in the world. If I pay attention, I might one day run the Pint Pot. Aunt Nettie said she can't live forever, so she wants someone who will be reliable enough to take over the business. It's been in our family a long time. I've already started coming up with ideas to expand it without alienating our longtime clientele. Working here is going to give me even more inspiration. And that way I can make sure the Pint Pot's professional relationships stay positive."

"How wonderful," Aunt Jinny declared. "And very wise of your aunt. I like to see businesses stay in the family." She gave Harriet a bright smile.

Harriet smiled back. How grateful she was to have been offered the opportunity to take over her grandad's veterinary practice in this delightful seaside community.

When Phoebe strolled away, offering sandwiches to others here and there, Harriet scanned the throng again for Van and Polly. Where were they? She'd begun to feel a twinge of misgiving. With everyone crowded together so tightly, perhaps she simply couldn't see them from where she was standing.

"I'm going to work my way to the other side of the parlor to see if Polly and Van are somewhere on that side of the room," Harriet said. "I know she wouldn't want to miss this. She's keen to explore the chamber down below. She told me so."

Will gave a nod. "I'll check around too. They might be helping Nettie make sure the families get all the right boxes and crates."

"Good idea," Aunt Jinny said. "I'll stay put and keep my eye out for them. Knowing Van, he's in that crowd around the refreshment table."

"It's not like Van to miss out on free food," Will agreed with a chuckle.

But Van wasn't near the table. Nor was Polly. Harriet knew her friend had been looking forward to the tea party. They'd discussed it briefly on Friday morning, when Harriet had filled Polly in on the discovery of the stairs inside the bench. Polly had been a rapt audience, demanding every single detail about the goods stored there and the odd door that led to the old smugglers' cave. So where was she?

Harriet stepped out into the corridor to try calling Polly. Perhaps she'd forgotten about the party. It wasn't likely—it seemed no one in town had talked about anything else since the Beems had made the announcement. But still, it wouldn't hurt to give Polly a reminder.

When her call went straight to voice mail, Harriet left a message. Then she decided to call Van. He didn't pick up either.

She sent Polly a text. YOU'RE MISSING ALL THE FUN. WHERE ARE YOU?

Fearing that there had indeed been a family emergency of some sort—she couldn't imagine another reason for Polly to miss an event she'd been so excited for—Harriet called the Thatcher family's landline. Perhaps something had happened to Polly's grandmother. The woman was quite elderly.

Before her mind could spiral down that particular path too far, the call was answered. "Thatcher residence."

"Hi, Mrs. Thatcher," Harriet said, trying to keep the worry out of her voice. Surely if something had happened to Callista, Polly's mother wouldn't sound so calm. "It's Harriet. I was wondering if you've seen Polly. I'm at the celebratory tea at the Quill and Scroll, and I don't see her anywhere. I know she was eager to explore the secret passageway underneath the inn, and I'm sure she'd enjoy seeing so many families being reunited with their family heirlooms after all these years. Did she forget?"

"Quite right, dear. Our Polly would love to explore those secret tunnels," Mrs. Thatcher agreed. "Always tagging along with her brothers when she was a young thing, refusing to be left out of any of their adventures. But Polly went away for the weekend. Didn't she tell you?"

Shock stole Harriet's breath. No, Polly hadn't mentioned going away for the weekend, and she always told Harriet where she was.

"I see," Harriet said. "Do you know where she went?"

"I'm sorry, but I don't. She packed a small suitcase and hurried off, blowing me a kiss as she darted out the door and insisting that I didn't fuss about it. I try to respect her as an adult, so I'm sure this is simply a spur-of-the-moment getaway and she'll tell us all about it when she gets back."

"I'm sure," Harriet echoed. "Thank you for telling me, Mrs. Thatcher. Have a nice day."

"Enjoy your tea," Mrs. Thatcher chirped merrily. She hung up.

Harriet rejoined her aunt in the parlor and explained her phone call to the Thatcher residence. "Don't you think that's odd?"

Aunt Jinny shrugged. "Not really. Plans change. This isn't the first time Polly's done something impulsive. But she's not foolish or reckless, so I'm sure she's fine."

"No luck," Will said, ambling over with a tiny cheese tart.

"Apparently, Polly went away for the weekend," Harriet told him. Just then her cell phone pinged. She read the screen and breathed a sigh of relief. "It's a text from Polly. She's in some place called Gretna Green. That's in Scotland, right?"

Will choked on his tart. He and Aunt Jinny exchanged wide-eyed stares.

Frowning, Harriet glanced from one to the other. "What?"

"Don't you remember Gretna Green from all those Regency romances you read as a girl?" Aunt Jinny demanded. When Harriet shook her head, her aunt added, "It's where couples run off to elope."

Harriet felt her throat go dry. "Surely not!"

Will began to chuckle. His hazel eyes twinkled.

Aunt Jinny grinned from ear to ear. "I can believe it. It's not like they're underage or anything. And surely their families would approve. And it's so like Polly to want to surprise us all like this."

Harriet's phone pinged again. Another text from Polly, this one accompanied by a photo of her and Van, wearing brand-new wedding bands and effervescent smiles. Harriet's heart began to race as she read the words not once, but twice. Happy tears filled her eyes, but she quickly wiped them away. It wouldn't do to be seen crying in public, especially over an announcement that was not hers to make. Clearing her throat, Harriet gave a watery sniff and read the text to Will and Aunt Jinny. "'Married yesterday. Back on Tuesday. I cleared your calendar for tomorrow. Wish us happiness.'"

Aunt Jinny's smile softened. "It's so sweet and old-fashioned."

"And romantic too," Will added. He reached for Harriet's hand and gave it a squeeze. "Perhaps we should have considered that."

She squeezed back. She thought of the young couple who'd run away to be married, and toyed with the idea of doing the same. It would certainly reduce the stress of planning a big wedding. However, she quickly dismissed the idea. "I can see the appeal, but I don't think my parents would ever recover. Besides, that doesn't feel like the right choice for us, does it?"

He kissed her temple. "Definitely not. What's right for us is what we're doing."

Glad they were on the same page as usual, Harriet leaned her head against his shoulder with a sigh. Her dear friends had tied the knot, and she sent up a silent prayer that they'd have a long and happy life together.

Aunt Jinny broke into her reverie. "Polly and Van married. We must hold a reception for the newlyweds when they get back. And what about a bridal shower? People will want to celebrate their nuptials." She glanced around the parlor, which was less crowded now as people began leaving, eager no doubt to explore the contents of the long-lost trunks, boxes, and chests. "What a day this has been. I do love happy endings, don't you?"

Harriet smiled at Will, who returned it with a silent promise in his eyes. "Yes," she said. "And happy beginnings too."

FROM THE AUTHOR

Dear Reader,

I hope you've enjoyed the further adventures of Harriet Bailey and her friends and family in White Church Bay. Recently, a reader of this series told me how much she likes Harriet. I like Harriet too. Don't you? She's a woman with remarkable common sense and compassion—for both people and animals.

In many ways, Harriet reminds me of my sister Sandy, who happens to be a certified animal rehabilitator. Over the years, she has cared for many injured and orphaned animals, including hundreds of fawns. Like Jane Birtwhistle, Sandy usually has lots of cats and kittens at her place for which she tries to find suitable forever homes. Ducks, geese, wolves, foxes, prairie dogs, kestrels, and owls—one never knows what you'll find at her house if you stop by. One year, she took on the responsibility of bottle-feeding all sorts of zoo-born cubs: baby bears, tigers, lions, and leopards. My teenage son spent a week with her, bottle-feeding tiger cubs around the clock. Boy, did he ever enjoy writing his back-to-school "What I did over summer vacation" essay that year!

Sandy's a walking resource on all animal-related matters. I know I can always pick up the phone and ask questions like, "Can cats get sunburned from sitting on the windowsill?" and "Do goats really eat nails and rusty tin cans?" Sandy always knows the answer. If she doesn't, she has plenty of veterinarian friends who do.

Thanks for reading my second novel in the Mysteries of Cobble Hill series. I hope you'll stay tuned for more adventures with Harriet, Will, Polly, and the other friendly folks of White Church Bay.

Warmly,
Shirley Raye Redmond

ABOUT THE AUTHOR

Shirley Raye Redmond has received numerous awards for both her women's fiction and children's books. Her devotions have appeared in multiple volumes of Guideposts' *All God's Creatures* and *Walking in Grace,* and she has enjoyed writing several mysteries for Guideposts' Savannah Secrets, and Secrets from Grandma's Attic series. Shirley Raye has been married for more than fifty years to her college sweetheart. They live in the scenic mountains of northern New Mexico and have two adult children and five grandchildren. Shirley Raye admits to being an Anglophile. She loves Atlantic puffins, Earl Grey tea, English toffee, and Arundel Castle….*and* has been known to eat Tiptree's lemon curd with a spoon straight out of the jar!

TRUTH BEHIND THE FICTION

It is well known that the Nazis were notorious for stealing artwork, jewelry, and other valuables as they conquered one European nation after another. It all began in 1933, when they began stealing from Jewish German citizens. They didn't just steal from wealthy people—they robbed everyone, taking clocks, watches, vehicles, books, musical instruments, and financial assets. Often, the Nazis seized homes, leaving displaced families on the streets or sending them to the dreaded concentration camps.

As they moved across Europe, the Nazis helped themselves to anything they wanted, including food, livestock, and harvested crops. It was not uncommon for people to try hiding their treasured possessions from the plundering Nazis.

British Prime Minister Winston Churchill was concerned about losing the UK's cultural treasures too. Determined to protect the masterpieces at the National Gallery, Churchill ordered those in charge to "hide them in caves and cellars, but not one picture shall leave this island." The beautiful Elgin Marbles were hidden in a subway station, and other British treasures were stashed in underground mines.

Although I'm not sure how many British citizens hid their prized possessions in smugglers' caves like the residents of White

Church Bay in this fictional story, many did bury their belongings in their gardens, in crypts, and other secret hiding places. I can only imagine how many families unintentionally lost family heirlooms this way, and I pray that we never face such a horrific situation again.

YORKSHIRE YUMMIES

Mrs. Truelove's Gooseberry Pie

Here's the pie that Harriet so enjoyed at the Truelove farm.

Ingredients:
Pastry for double-crust 9-inch pie
3 cups gooseberries
1½ cups sugar
3 tablespoons quick-cooking tapioca
¼ teaspoon salt
2 tablespoons butter

Directions:
1. Line 9-inch pie plate with pastry.
2. Crush ½ cup gooseberries.
3. Combine crushed gooseberries with sugar, tapioca, and salt.
4. Cook and stir until mixture thickens and boils.
5. Add 2½ cups whole gooseberries. Pour into pastry shell.
6. Cover with top of pastry.
7. Dot pastry top with butter.
8. Adjust and seal top crust, cutting slits for steam to escape.
9. Bake in oven at 400 degrees for 30 to 40 minutes until golden brown.
10. Serve warm and enjoy!

Read on for a sneak peek of another exciting book in the Mysteries of Cobble Hill Farm *series!*

Stray From The Fold

by Cynthia Ruchti

Pastor Fitzwilliam "Will" Knight reached into a turquoise-striped box and gently lifted out the most beautiful cupcake Dr. Harriet Bailey had ever seen. His hazel eyes watched her carefully for her reaction to the small cake in a turquoise baking paper, lavishly decorated with pale yellow frosting.

"This is what you're suggesting for the wedding cake?" She made sure her amusement didn't come across as shock. "It's a bit small, isn't it? How will it feed all our guests?"

"We'd have a much larger version, of course." He held his hand over the cupcake to give her a visual. "Or a tower of these fairy cakes, perhaps?" Fairy cake was the common term for cupcake in England.

"Where did you get this? I haven't seen anything like it in White Church Bay." She scooted aside papers to create a larger free spot on the clinic's reception desk, far from where a cat crate or birdcage might ever sit.

Will's face registered his delight. "The Happy Cup Tearoom and Bakery is capable of making anything we choose," he reminded her. "They can also make the cake and frosting whatever colors we want. What do you think?"

Harriet rotated the small, scalloped plate in her hands as a kennel club judge might examine the best of show. "It's flawless. Elegant, but not over the top."

"That's why I like it. We're not over-the-top people."

"How can you say that when I'm wearing my best shoes?" Harriet tapped the toes of her wellies against the floor, offering proof with her footwear. She would have left them on the mat at the door as usual, but the week had been so dry that she wasn't worried about whether she'd track anything in.

"Forgive me. I meant no offense. Does the cake meet with your approval for our wedding?" Will asked.

"The cake is really lovely, Will," Harriet assured him. "And I like the idea of individual cupcakes for our guests, with perhaps a larger one for the bride and groom. I'd like to follow the tradition of saving some to share on our first anniversary."

"Excellent idea, Harriet. That's step one—the design."

She chuckled. "I didn't realize there were steps. What's step two?"

"Taste." He retrieved a turquoise fork from the box, cut off a bite of cake, and offered it to her. "Earl Grey sponge with seedless blackberry jam and lemon frosting."

She closed her eyes, savoring the flavors. The cake itself tasted beautifully of the hearty, slightly citrusy tea, which emphasized the tart lemon in the frosting. The tangy blackberry added another note without overriding any of it. "Oh, Will, it's incredible!"

"I think so too."

"Have I interrupted an important wedding conversation? Should I come back later?" Polly Thatcher-Worthington leaned against the doorframe, grinning.

"Not at all. In fact, it's just the kind of thing we need the matron of honor's input on," Harriet replied.

"Is this fairy cake for love or for the wedding?" Polly asked as she approached.

"Both," Will and Harriet answered in unison then smiled at each other.

If Harriet had known such happiness was possible...what would she have done? Moved to England sooner to take over her grandfather's veterinary practice, perhaps learning from him directly before his passing? Would she have stopped resisting her heart's tug toward Will months earlier and hushed the inner insecurity that warned her to keep her distance? Yes and yes. But she supposed everything had happened in God's perfect timing.

Swooning over lemon frosting would have to bow to the need of the moment. "Do you have time to place our order with the Happy Cup, Will?"

"I do." He winked. "Good practice, that. 'I do.'"

She shook her head, grinning. "Thank you. At last count, we have one hundred and fifty RSVPs."

"What do you think, then? Order enough to serve two hundred? I don't mind a year's worth of leftovers in the freezer. I've been assured the cake will keep, as long as we store it properly."

"Sounds perfect. Thank you for taking care of that."

"You don't need to thank me. This is my wedding too, and there's a lot to be done. It shouldn't all fall to you."

A car pulled into the parking lot. Harriet peeked around Will to see if her suspicion was correct. "If you two will excuse me," she said, "I believe my first patient has shown up a little early. A much-loved cat named Millie has a suspicious growth on her abdomen. We noticed it on her last visit, but her owner, Estelle Payne, called yesterday to tell me she thinks it's grown bigger just over the last few days. I told her I'd see them first thing this morning before our scheduled appointments start to arrive for the day."

"Should I prepare the surgery?" Polly shed her light jacket and geared up for the workday as she spoke.

Harriet thought for a moment. "Let's get through the exam first. I should know fairly quickly whether we'll need to operate."

Will scooped up the bakery box and headed for the exit. "I'll leave you to the fun. And don't worry about the cake, Harriet. I won't eat any more until we can share it."

"Thanks, dear. Love you," Harriet called after him.

"Love you too," he said as the door swung shut.

Polly grinned at Harriet. "Is it my imagination, or did Will finally figure out how to be romantic?"

Harriet toed out of her wellies and slid into her work shoes. "I think he always knew the specific kind of romance that speaks to me. I am so blessed."

"We both are." Polly sighed. "Eloping was the right choice for Van and me, but cake like that might have changed my mind."

"You've been a newlywed for less than a month. It's not too late for cake," Harriet replied on her way to finish her prep.

With the cat's exam completed, Harriet braced herself for the discussion with Millie's owner.

"We won't have the results back from the regional lab for a week or more, but it looks suspiciously like a mast cell tumor, Estelle. But you know cats. They love to surprise us. And Millie just might."

"I'd rather she surprise me with a bulb from my garden, like she did yesterday. Not something serious."

"Before we let our concern get out of hand, let's wait on the results of the biopsy. Until then, the painkiller I've prescribed for Millie should ease her discomfort. And she may become even more fond of lap time than she was before. Polly will give you instructions for caring for the biopsy site."

"Thank you, Dr. Bailey. I appreciate your kindness. I've a wee gift for you." She extended a package wrapped in what Harriet recognized as a recent issue of the *Whitby Gazette*.

"Thank you, Estelle," Harriet said as she opened the package. "I'm touched by your generosity. A pair of mittens! How very thoughtful."

"Mittens? In July?"

Seated at her desk in her office, Harriet ran her hands over the cream-colored, deeply textured surface of the mittens. "Sheep wool. The real thing. They're so beautiful. Besides, it's not like mittens expire. These will be wonderful this winter."

"Well, you know knitters," Polly said. "They can't really help themselves. What's the saying? 'I could stop any time. I just choose not to'?"

"That's another topic entirely, but yes, I can see the tendency in knitters too."

"Mittens in July is something I never would have thought of."

"They're beautifully made," Harriet went on. "With damp weather always around the bend here, I may be able to use them sooner than I expect."

"One never knows," Polly said, affecting an attitude of someone three times her age. "Ah, there's the phone. I'll get it." She headed for the reception desk as Harriet's aunt, Genevieve Garrett, entered.

"Hello, Aunt Jinny. How are you?" Harriet was delighted to see her. Any room felt brighter with Aunt Jinny's presence.

"Busy, much like you are, I imagine. The summer crowds are prone to need a vet as well as a physician's comments on whether their mysterious rash is poison ivy. More are traveling with pets and service animals than ever before, aren't they?"

"They certainly seem to be. What can I do for you?"

Aunt Jinny tapped a file folder in her hand. "I have your lab results from your NHS annual physical."

Was it her imagination, or had Aunt Jinny's eyebrows lifted higher than normal, toward her strawberry-blond hairline? As a healthcare provider, even if Harriet's patients were of the mammal, aviary, and reptilian nature, she was required to remain current with her license and her personal health checks. "And?"

"All good."

Harriet hadn't been holding her breath. "Good" was the expected response.

"Except for one small detail."

That was unexpected. "Which detail?"

"Your blood pressure, my dear," Aunt Jinny said. "It's a Bailey trait. Generations of us have struggled with it."

Harriet snorted. "I'm too young for blood pressure issues. I'm not even in my midthirties. What young people do you know who have blood pressure problems?"

"Ones who carry undue stress or are related to this family."

A sudden chorus of bird calls, barks, and meows rose from the reception room. *Right on cue.* Stress? Couldn't be.

"All right. What do you suggest—cut down on salt except for the chips at Cliffside Chippy? Drink more water?" She hefted her ever-present water jug to emphasize that she was already on the case. "If you've seen me wrestle a lamb through a birth canal, you know I don't need to add more aerobic exercise."

Aunt Jinny crossed her arms over her lab coat. "Knitting, actually." She eyed the mittens on Harriet's desk. "Have you started already?"

Harriet grabbed the mittens and stuffed them in her roomy lab coat pocket. "No. These are a gift from a grateful animal owner. Really, Aunt Jinny? Knitting? With this crazy on-call schedule and a wedding to plan? I hardly have time to commit to a new hobby."

"That's all the more reason for you to do it. I'm prescribing regular doses of time to sit and knit. I'd give you the option to read instead, but, knowing you, you'd read veterinary journals and turn your downtime into more work. So knitting it is. It has similar effects on the mind and body as meditation, but I know you'd never be able to sit quietly without doing something with your hands."

Harriet sighed. For the life of her, she couldn't think of a reasonable argument against it. She'd tried knitting the previous December and maintained a passing interest in it, but she hadn't had time to dedicate to it. She still didn't.

"Food for thought," Aunt Jinny said as she turned to leave. Then she raised her index finger as if adding an important point. "*Low-salt* food for thought."

Harriet would have tossed a comeback her way if Polly hadn't filled the door, her eyes wider than normal. "Doc Bailey, you're needed in the car park. Stat."

Harriet took the side door to avoid the pets and owners who waited for their nonemergency appointments. She quickly walked around the corner of the building and saw a dour sixtysomething man standing beside a pickup truck, one strap of his overalls undone and hanging over his barrel chest. She strode up to him and extended her hand. "Good morning, Alfred," she said. "What brings you here?"

Alfred Ramshaw lowered the tailgate of his pickup to reveal a goat sprawled in the bed. "I need you to tell me what caused this, and if you tell me it was Arlene Pendergrasp, you'll not find me arguing."

"Oh dear. Is he gone?" Arlene's last name was Pendergraf, not Pendergrasp, but this hardly seemed the time to point that out.

The goat raised his head and twitched one foot as if to convince Harriet he was still kicking, literally and figuratively.

"Tell me what happened to him," the man growled. "I've never seen an animal so sick."

Harriet pulled disposable gloves from her pocket and climbed into the truck bed.

"Wish I'd had a pair of gloves. You think he's contagious to people? Or contaminated? What if it's nuclear fallout from some unfriendly country's testing?"

Harriet swallowed her laughter. He was being serious. "I'm fairly confident it isn't radiation sickness." She did her best to examine the limp goat, searching for a wound or other evidence. Harriet palpated his abdomen. Most animals would flinch at the very least or try to wiggle free from her grasp. Nothing. He smelled oddly foul, more so than an average goat. "He might have been struck by lightning, I suppose."

"Ain't seen lightning in more than a fortnight. Can't be that, Doc." Alfred shook his head as if that should have gone without saying.

"I need to make a more thorough examination and run tests."

"I'd think less of you if you didn't," he said, his voice less gruff than it had been. He obviously cared about his animals.

"What made you mention Arlene Pendergraf?"

"If anyone were up to no good in Yorkshire, it would be her." The gruffness was back in full force. "I think she's up to something."

"Why is that?" Harriet felt along the goat's spine for misalignment, but it seemed fine. Her relief was something she didn't dare express to the worried farmer.

"I got another goat who's unwell. Not this bad, but she's breathing like she grew up in a coal mine. I can't afford to lose her, or this one. And I've been seeing more than one crazy squirrel near the trees by my stone fence, the one that separates my land from Pretendergraf's. Maybe she infected the squirrels with something, and they're spreading the plague. If what ails this goat is spreading to my herd—" He turned his face away.

Harriet laid a hand on his shoulder. "I understand, Alfred. If it helps, I think he's stable for right now. I need to get him into the kennels until I see to the scheduled patients waiting for me inside and can devote my full attention to him."

"I can haul him there." Before Harriet could reply, Alfred lifted the goat. He grunted and struggled but managed to carry his goat all the way to the kennels in back.

Harriet bid him goodbye with a promise to let him know what she discovered with a full examination. The fact that he had more than one ailing animal with different symptoms—to say nothing of "crazy" squirrels—told Harriet that this was no ordinary ailment. Diagnosing and mystery-solving were often separated by a fine line. It seemed she'd just been invited to do both.

As his truck rolled out of the parking lot, she turned her attention to the sounds of a dog disagreement in the clinic behind her.

Harriet stuck her hands in her pockets as she made her way back toward the door. In the left pocket, her fingers touched the beautiful mittens from Estelle. "Knitting. Sure, Aunt Jinny. That's the answer to all my problems."

A NOTE FROM THE EDITORS

We hope you enjoyed another exciting volume in the Mysteries of Cobble Hill Farm series, published by Guideposts. For over seventy-five years, Guideposts, a nonprofit organization, has been driven by a vision of a world filled with hope. We aspire to be the voice of a trusted friend, a friend who makes you feel more hopeful and connected.

By making a purchase from Guideposts, you join our community in touching millions of lives, inspiring them to believe that all things are possible through faith, hope, and prayer. Your continued support allows us to provide uplifting resources to those in need. Whether through our communities, websites, apps, or publications, we inspire our audiences, bring them together, and comfort, uplift, entertain, and guide them. Visit us at guideposts.org to learn more.

We would love to hear from you. Write us at Guideposts, P.O. Box 5815, Harlan, Iowa 51593 or call us at (800) 932-2145. Did you love *Of Bats and Belfries*? Leave a review for this product on guideposts.org/shop. Your feedback helps others in our community find relevant products.

Find inspiration, find faith, find Guideposts.
Shop our best sellers and favorites at
guideposts.org/shop
Or scan the QR code to go directly to our Shop.

Loved Mysteries of Cobble Hill Farm? Check out some other Guideposts mystery series! Visit https://www.shopguideposts.org/fiction-books/mystery-fiction.html for more information.

SECRETS FROM GRANDMA'S ATTIC

Life is recorded not only in decades or years, but in events and memories that form the fabric of our being. Follow Tracy Doyle, Amy Allen, and Robin Davisson, the granddaughters of the recently deceased centenarian, Pearl Allen, as they explore the treasures found in the attic of Grandma Pearl's Victorian home, nestled near the banks of the Mississippi in Canton, Missouri. Not only do Pearl's descendants uncover a long-buried mystery at every attic exploration, they also discover their grandmother's legacy of deep, abiding faith, which has shaped and guided their family through the years. These uncovered Secrets from Grandma's Attic reveal stories of faith, redemption, and second chances that capture your heart long after you turn the last page.

History Lost and Found
The Art of Deception
Testament to a Patriot
Buttoned Up

Pearl of Great Price
Hidden Riches
Movers and Shakers
The Eye of the Cat
Refined by Fire
The Prince and the Popper
Something Shady
Duel Threat
A Royal Tea
The Heart of a Hero
Fractured Beauty
A Shadowy Past
In Its Time
Nothing Gold Can Stay
The Cameo Clue
Veiled Intentions
Turn Back the Dial
A Marathon of Kindness
A Thief in the Night
Coming Home

More Great Mysteries Are Waiting for Readers Like *You*!

Whistle Stop Café

"Memories of a lifetime...I loved reading this story. Could not put the book down...." —ROSE H.

Mystery and WWII historical fiction fans will love these intriguing novels where two close friends piece together clues to solve mysteries past and present. Set in the real town of Dennison, Ohio, at a historic train depot where many soldiers set off for war, these stories are filled with faithful, relatable characters you'll love spending time with.

Extraordinary Women of the Bible

"This entire series is a wonderful read.... Gives you a better understanding of the Bible." —SHARON A.

Now, in these riveting stories, you can get to know the most extraordinary women of the Bible, from Rahab and Esther to Bathsheba, Ruth, and more. Each book perfectly combines biblical facts with imaginative storylines to bring these women to vivid life and lets you witness their roles in God's great plan. These stories reveal how we can find the courage and faith needed today to face life's trials and put our trust in God just as they did.

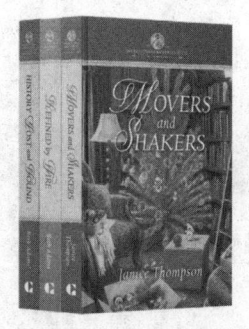

Secrets of Grandma's Attic

"I'm hooked from beginning to end. I love how faith, hope, and prayer are included...[and] the scripture references... in the book at the appropriate time each character needs help. —JACQUELINE

Take a refreshing step back in time to the real-life town of Canton, Missouri, to the late Pearl Allen's home. Hours of page-turning intrigue unfold as her granddaughters uncover family secrets and treasures in their grandma's attic. You'll love seeing how faith has helped shape Pearl's family for generations.

Learn More & Shop These Exciting Mysteries, Biblical Stories & Other Uplifting Fiction at **guideposts.org/fiction**